PET BLOGGING 101

HOW TO START A RIVETING PET BLOG AND GAIN LOYAL FOLLOWERS

WENDY VAN DE POLL

SPIRIT PAW PRESS, LLC

Pet Blogging 101:
How to Start a Riveting Pet Blog and
Gain Loyal Followers

Kindle and Softcover Editions
Copyright © 2019 Spirit Paw Press, LLC

All rights reserved. No part of this publication may be reproduced, distributed, or transmitted in any form or by any means, including photocopying, recording, or other electronic or mechanical methods, without the prior written permission of the publisher, except in the case of brief quotations embodied in reviews and certain other non-commercial uses permitted by copyright law.

Published by Spirit Paw Press, LLC, Concord, NH, 03303

Publisher's Cataloging-in-Publication Data
provided by Five Rainbows Cataloging Services

Names: Van de Poll, Wendy, author.
Title: Pet blogging 101 : how to start a riveting pet blog and gain loyal followers / Wendy Van de Poll.
Description: Concord, NH : Spirit Paw Press, 2019. | Series: Pet business, bk. 1. | Also available in ebook format.
Identifiers: ISBN 978-1-7324375-3-1 (softcover)
Subjects: LCSH: Blogs. | Pets. | Online authorship. | WordPress (Electronic resource) | Small business--Management. | BISAC: COMPUTERS / Web / Blogging. | PETS / General. | BUSINESS & ECONOMICS / Small Business.
Classification: LCC PN171.O55 .V36 2019 (print) | LCC PN171.O55 (ebook) | DDC 302.23/1--dc23.

THANK YOU

A Free Gift

Thank you for purchasing *Pet Blogging 101: How to Start a Riveting Pet Blog and Gain Loyal Followers*. To show my appreciation, I am offering a **Free Gift** to help you start your blog!

A Free Downloadable Checklist:

Create Your Winning Pet Website or Blog

Your link to receive your Free Gift!
https://bit.ly/2Zu0KRq

For all the animals that grace my life. You are behind this mission as you are with all of my work.

CONTENTS

Introduction — xi

Section I
CREATING YOUR BLOG

1. Courage and Inspiration — 3
2. Finding Your Niche and Appealing to Followers — 12

Section II
SETTING UP YOUR BLOG

3. Finding a Home for Your Blog — 33
4. WordPress Bootcamp — 46
5. Creating Winning Content — 63

Section III
GROWING YOUR BLOG FOR SUCCESS

6. Getting Social with Social Media — 83
7. Get Them to Come Back! — 95
8. Monetizing Your Blog — 104

Pep Talk! — 116
Glossary — 118
Resources — 121
Acknowledgements — 124
About the Author — 125
Thank You! — 126
Also By Wendy Van de Poll — 127

INTRODUCTION

Do you have the yearning to start a blog about pets, but don't know where to begin? Would you like to know how to get from your awesome idea to creating a successful blog? Is the thought of getting started overwhelming you?

The truth is that your idea is the seed that can grow into something great if you plant it.

You already made the first step by picking up this book. This book is your ultimate starting point. It contains what you need to know about starting your pet blog. I have outlined the steps from SEO to WordPress to affiliate marketing that you must take to make your blog a reality.

Don't feel that you lack the knowledge or skills to be a successful blogger, because I have included what you need to know to get started is in these pages. If you follow the chapters from start to finish, you will have created a unique brand that will inspire you.

But first you may be wondering what a blog is and how it is different than a website.

A *blog*, according to Merriam-Webster Dictionary, is a website that contains online personal reflections, comments, and often hyperlinks, videos, and photographs provided by the writer. A *website* is a group of World Wide Web pages usually containing hyperlinks to each other and made available online by an individual, company, educational institution, government, or organization. Websites host blogs.

These are terms often used interchangeably. But for the purpose of this book, I will use blog. My advice is to not get distracted by the correct use of blog or website.

As a professional pet blogger for twenty-plus years and the founder of

INTRODUCTION

five blogs (two of which I created and then sold), I have the experience necessary to teach you how to blog.

Blogging is one of my passions, and helping people start their pet blog is inspiring. Guiding people who have the passion to share their ideas, knowledge, and expertise to help animals and pet lovers is an amazing experience. I want to help you feel the same.

If you want to create a blog, then you can do it. With this book, you will be able to create a riveting blog that will reach and attract many readers.

As you grow your readership, you will also grow as a person. I cannot stress enough how rewarding blogging is, as you reach people and change their lives.

You will meet many great people, you will make a difference in many lives, and you may even generate a nice income. Blogging is worth it. It just takes a few skills and some hard work to get going.

The most important thing is to be yourself. Find your voice and write what you want to write about. Share the photos that you love. Even feel free to make some mistakes and learn from them.

As you start this journey, you will learn many things, and you will perform the necessary research that will make you an expert in your particular pet niche. Be open to growth and you will find that your blog is a fantastic vehicle to things you never imagined learning and accomplishing.

My twenty-year success rate with pet blogging has enriched my professional and personal life on many levels. My sites have rated well with Google, my client base increased whenever I post an article, and I am seen as an expert in the pet loss genre.

When I created and sold my two sites: natural-pet-essentials.com and chronic-pain-management.com (not a pet site), the pet industry was gaining momentum. I saw the potential for growth in the pet blogging industry. I didn't quit. I kept going.

INTRODUCTION

My hope is that you keep going with your idea. With this book, you will be able to create your riveting and unique blog that will help people and animals around the world. You will change lives and gain an online community that will enrich your life by doing something meaningful.

Don't wait for this opportunity. Are you ready to start your pet blog? Then let's get started!

Affiliate links are present at the end of this book. This means if you purchase the product, I receive a small commission (which helps me greatly as an author.) You are not charged more because of the affiliate link. In fact, sometimes there is even a small discount. I have personally tested all affiliate products mentioned. I would never recommend something I didn't love.

I

CREATING YOUR BLOG

1

COURAGE AND INSPIRATION
Fortune sides with him who dares. — Virgil

You want to start a pet blog. I can't commend your bravery enough. It takes a lot of courage to put yourself out there in front of fans and critics alike, to share your thoughts with a blog, and to try to generate income in a nonconventional way. But that courage pays off, and the rewards of writing a pet blog can be monumental.

All pet lovers share something in common: a deep love for pets and a desire to be good pet parents. As you start your blog, you will realize you have a larger audience than you may have previously thought.

The Internet Age has made it possible to connect with other similar people more easily than ever. Your blog will have a home in an online pet community, where other people will warm your heart with their stories and pictures, just as you warm theirs.

It is normal to be anxious whenever you attempt something new. As you begin your blog, you may wonder, "Will anyone care what I have to say? Do I even have the skills to do this? What the heck am I getting myself into?" You may also wonder, "What should I write about?"

WILL ANYONE CARE?

First, there is no need to worry. People *will* care about what you have to say. Pet lovers are forever researching and looking to connect with like-minded people.

You will have an audience of dedicated readers, as long as you stay true to your voice and focus on delivering meaningful pet-related content. This book will show you how to find a niche that you can use to reach followers, as well as how to appeal to your readers by being yourself.

The Internet is quite saturated with content, and you will have competition. But if you stay true to your unique voice, you will stand out from the crowd naturally.

No one can offer just what you have to offer. Being unique is critical. You must offer readers something that they can't get in other blogs.

When I got started with natural-pet-essentials.com twenty years ago, I was scared to put myself out there. I was an animal lover with no official nutritional training.

However, what I had going for me was I lived a natural and holistic lifestyle. I was a canine and equine massage therapist, I prepared my dogs' food (before raw feeding was discovered), and I treated them with acupuncture, herbs, and homeopathy.

I researched everything I could find about taking care of the body, mind, and spirit of animals. And this, my friends, was the material for my blog. I used my unique voice and my passion for a holistic lifestyle to make my blog successful.

My site gained momentum fast. I was affiliate marketing, offering freebies (Chapter 8), and producing a new article every day.

When I sold this site, I was very proud of what I created.

DO YOU HAVE THE SKILLS?

You already possess some of the skills necessary for launching a successful pet blog. Your love for pets, your knowledge, and your life experiences—these are three skills that will make your blog flourish.

You don't have to be some rock-star writer with twenty published books or a pet expert with a veterinary degree to make it as a pet blogger. As long as you deliver on your idea and research your claims, your blog will be able to offer something to the world.

Think about the stories you want to share. No one else on this planet possesses those exact stories. No one has your pets, or your pictures, either. Sharing these snippets of your life with your pets and creating a little (or big) community of pet lovers will brighten the lives of so many people.

If you know about home remedies and tricks for caring for pets, how to run a business, or like to review products, you already have tons of useful content that other pet owners will want (Chapters 5 and 8).

Whatever your blog is about, this is your space to share what you have to offer others. Make it yours and truly yours!

Computer skills can scare some people off from blogging. If you know how to visit websites and type, that is a good start. You don't need to know fancy code to create a blog. I will teach you how to basically use the software that I love that handles all of the complex back-end stuff for you.

All you have to do is download the software, pick your design, input your content, and register and publish the blog. The rest is handled for you by your host and your WordPress suite (Chapter 4).

Owning your voice is the single most important thing you can do to stand out from the competition. However, there is obviously more to it.

No one will read your blog if no one knows about it. You can have the most wonderful content, but if you don't put it in front of people, you won't get readers.

Never fear, though, because this book will show you how to rank higher on search engines, how to use social media to build a brand people know about, and how to reach and incur followers. You must put in the work to put yourself out there, but I can promise you it is worth it.

WHAT ARE YOU GETTING YOURSELF INTO?

Yes, a blog is hard work. As a blogger, I cannot lie and claim that blogging is easy, passive income. You must post often, you must market yourself, and you must create an attractive site that is both convenient and accessible for readers.

Creating your blog is probably the most time-consuming part. A blog also requires ongoing upkeep and maintenance.

But all of this is work that can be both rewarding and relatively straightforward. You get to write about what you love! You can work from anywhere, anytime! And you can find new colleagues through the community you create. Your blog will be a reflection of what you love to do. And that is—talk about animals!

Blogs do require some patience, as well. It can take a while to build a following. Don't let impatience get the best of you because all good things come with time.

If you are dedicated and keep working, you will see a return. You might have zero readers for your first post; keep posting. You might not get anyone signing up for your email list; revisit your blog and tweak your description or content to offer your readers more of what they want.

To make money through your blog, you can use several different avenues. I cover many of them in Chapter 8. You can use the blog to market your own line or business, or you can use affiliate marketing to get paid by companies when readers click on your links. You will find that this is an excellent revenue stream. Once you get yourself in front of readers, you open the doors too many potential lucrative money-making opportunities.

When I first started writing, I started on a whim. I wasn't sure if anyone would want to read my work or if anyone would care about what I had to say. My blog took off, however, and I was shocked to discover that one day I was very successful.

Treating your blog as a whim is a good way to start because it removes the fear. Don't think of it as a matter of life or death. Think of it as a fun new venture. You will be surprised by the success that makes all of your hard work and writing pay off.

It is a shame to let your dream die because you are afraid. It is far better to try; the only failure is not trying at all! While you may not know what you are getting into, I promise it is fun and rewarding. Try it out and maybe you will find that starting a blog is something you enjoy.

WHAT SHOULD YOU WRITE ABOUT?

Now that you have the courage to make your blog a success, you need to work on finding inspiration. You are likely already inspired to create a blog and make money through it. But what if you lack inspiration on what to write about?

It is okay to feel uninspired sometimes. Inspiration can come from many places. Read other blogs or books. Watch a movie or take a walk. Talk to people about ideas. Think about causes you care about and things you would like to change in the pet world through education. Ideas will come to you.

Be sure to write all of your ideas down so you don't forget anything. It is a common saying that if you forget an idea, it wasn't that good of an idea to begin with. In the flurry of busyness that is my life, I cannot say that is true at all.

It is easy to forget things when you are busy or when you have many ideas, but each idea can become something great if acted upon. Always carry a little notebook with you and jot down ideas as they come to you.

My inspirations come when I am walking my dog in nature. Nature clears my mind and allows me to think creatively. I record my ideas on my phone when I get an idea or a brainstorm.

Using your pets as inspiration is also a great way to find things to write about. Think about your love for them and what you want to share with the world about them. Think about how you can make a difference for other people and other pets. That love will show in your writing and your photos, which can certainly appeal to followers.

Don't be scared to put your ideas out there. Don't feel that something you want to write about is stupid or a poor idea. And certainly, don't throttle your ideas by worrying about whether or not they appeal to followers!

This blog is your little space in the world. You can fill it with whatever you want. Someone will appreciate it.

The most successful blogs offer useful information. You might offer reviews of pet products to help other pet owners research and buy products. Companies will also pay you to review their products, and you will get tons of free products from sponsors!

Or you might offer instructional videos, such as how to potty train your puppy or how to get pet odors out of carpets. You might offer very specific educational information on certain breeds of lizards and how to care for them.

Drawing on your expertise and life experiences, documenting your trial-and-error discoveries, and passing on research you have performed can make you extremely successful.

This is because you are teaching people things they don't know. When they scour the Internet for answers or start preliminary research before they bring a new pet into their home—they will find you and you will will be there to help them.

However, there are also many successful blogs dedicated to simply warming people's hearts. These blogs share stories about the joys and trials of pet ownership.

Think of the book and movie *Marley and Me*, wherein the author documented his experience with a very rambunctious puppy. The book became a bestseller, and the movie grossed millions.

Just sharing your stories and photos will appeal to many readers who want to find someone to relate to. Pet lovers around the world will enjoy reading what you have to share.

There is no need to find something that is trending and then force yourself to fit into that little box. You can operate on a completely original idea and find great success. You never know what people will like until you try it.

Cramming yourself into a niche that you don't actually like will not bring the rewards that creating your own niche or writing in a niche that you enjoy will bring. Don't just do what is popular. Do what is you!

WRAP-UP

In this chapter, you have learned how to find courage and inspiration. You have also learned some answers to your biggest anxiety questions.

The basic message is this: You can do it! And once you do, you will be very happy with the results. A blog is extremely rewarding. You will find that your blog is a place to express yourself, make a difference in the world, and maybe make you some passive income.

Don't worry about not being good enough. You are good enough. What you don't know, you can learn. Many more people will love your voice than you realize.

Just be yourself and write about what you enjoy. Don't be afraid to share your thoughts with the world. You will gain an audience because you will stand out from the competition with the inherent uniqueness of your brand.

Plus, you will learn a lot and grow as a person. You will virtually meet many great people, many of whom will become great lifelong followers. All of these things make blogging an enriching and rewarding undertaking that anyone can accomplish.

Use the action steps at the end of this chapter to get you started with finding your courage and inspiration.

The next chapter will focus on finding your niche and appealing to followers. You will learn about your niche, how to title your blog, how to write to your demographic, and how to stand out from the competition. In addition, I provide the bare-bones basics of SEO, though I cover this more extensively in Chapters 3 and 6.

YOUR FIRST THREE ACTION STEPS

Listed are the steps I covered in this chapter. Use the action steps as a checklist as you proceed with creating your blog. Refer back in this chapter to gain more detail when you are ready for the tasks outlined below.

STEP 1: GATHER COURAGE

Let go of fear, and let courage fill your soul. This blog is your baby. You don't need to be some expert or a professional writer to make it beautiful. Your knowledge and experience are already enough. The rest you can learn with this book.

STEP 2: SEEK INSPIRATION

Draw on your love of pets or your enthusiasm for pet care. Look to your experiences and stories. Consider the change you wish to make in the pet world. Your love of pets, your life experiences, and your passions are all valuable sources of inspiration that can get you far.

STEP 3: SET A CLEAR PURPOSE IN MIND

This step comes in handy as you move to the next chapter. You must determine what your blog will be about and what you want to achieve with it. That will drive everything you do in your blog, and it will also help you find a niche and a readership. Plus, having a purpose helps motivate you, so even when you feel like giving up, you keep going to reach that big goal in your mind.

2

FINDING YOUR NICHE AND APPEALING TO FOLLOWERS

If everybody is doing it one way, there's a good chance you can find your niche by going exactly in the opposite direction. — Sam Walton

When starting a blog, you need to establish a niche, or a purpose. Think of it as if you are etching out your own little part of the blogging world, a place where your followers and you feel comfortable.

Your niche needs to be something that you can write about with confidence. It needs to be something that enriches the lives of your followers, making them want to come back for more. Furthermore, it needs to be something that you enjoy writing about and your readers enjoy reading about.

After all, you won't want to stick to writing a blog on topics that you find boring, and your lack of enthusiasm will show to your followers.

Every blog needs a definitive purpose to drive its content and attract followers. The purpose needs to be reflected in your title and your overall content. This hardly means that you need to stick to writing about one specific brand of pet food, because you will rapidly run out of content that way.

It just means that your articles should reflect the purpose overall, such as a series of articles about home remedies for common pet maladies or a blog focused on providing pet product reviews.

This brings me to a very important point: Don't pigeonhole yourself! Picking a topic that is too narrow will consequently narrow down your readership. A blog about one type of turtle food is a good example of how you can pick a topic that is just too specific.

With your content and your title, you attract readers. If you pick a topic that is too small, you run out of things to write about and people lose interest as they realize they have reaped all of the information your blog has to offer.

Then, if you try to expand your topic, you find that you don't attract readers because your title and previous content makes them expect only one thing. Avoid being too specific. Leave some wiggle room to expand into new realms of content to appeal to more people.

However, you also don't want to pick a topic that is too broad. "All things pets" could be too broad, for instance. If you have too general or broad of a topic, your readers won't know what to expect. They will ask, "Will this blogger ever post anything relevant to me? I can't tell, so I'm going to move on to a more specific blog."

Make it clear that your blog is about dogs, or turtles, or pet product reviews. Show readers exactly what to expect and then deliver.

For instance, my blog, Center for Pet Loss Grief, has a specific theme: the grief that comes with losing a pet. It is reflected clearly in the title. People know what to expect when they read my blog, and they choose to come to my blog when they need support after losing a pet.

This topic is not too broad, but it encompasses a wide variety of points and subtopics, which make it an engaging resource to my readers. It appeals to a big demographic, as well, since many people go through the tragic loss of a pet in their lifetimes. More on demographics later in this chapter.

The adage, "Write what you know," does have some truth to it. You don't want to write about something you have no idea about because you won't be able to offer as much information to your readers or engage yourself.

However, I don't think this is always true. Life is about learning and broadening your horizons. You can always do research and learn more about new topics that you can then share with your readers.

Make your blog a place where you learn and grow with your followers, creating a harmonious educational space that brings you and your readers together into a community.

Start with a topic that you know something about and want to write about; then expand it with research, interviews, and enlightening links to other articles.

The best way to find your niche is to draw from your own life experience, strengths, and interests. If you are an avid amphibian owner, you probably want to write about caring for amphibians. You already know a lot about the topic and have some personal stories to share with readers.

But you also have a lot that you can learn on the topic. Look at what you love about pets, what you want to share with the world, and what you feel you can comfortably write about. Chances are, you already have an idea of the topic you want to write about. Now it's time to determine how to present that topic in a palatable way that is neither too vague nor too specific.

If you are like me, you are an idea person. I am always full of dynamic ideas, and I sometimes find myself waking up at night and scrambling out of bed to jot some new idea down before it is lost in the haze of sleep. That is always a great quality, but sometimes you have to write your ideas down and then pare them down to find the one that fits a solid purpose.

If your mind is swirling with ideas for your blog, write them all down and sort them into categories based on the overall topic. Figure out the purpose of your blog and then only expand on the ideas that fit into that purpose.

Ideas that are too incongruent with your niche should probably get a separate blog of their own. It would be odd to start a blog on canine nutrition, only to throw in a series of articles about snake handling.

There is no reason why you can't have several blogs on different topics! But it is a mistake to jumble tons of different topics and ideas into a single blog. It appears disorganized and, again, too broad.

It all boils down to readership, the main reason you are blogging in the first place. You want to appeal to specific people and appear in the search engine list when people search for a certain topic that applies to their needs. Fitting into a good, solid niche that certain people find relevant will earn you more loyal followers.

FINDING YOUR PEOPLE

A major part (perhaps the main part) of deciding your niche and directing the content of your blog involves finding your demographic. Who are you writing to?

Obviously, you are writing a pet blog, so your audience will be comprised of pet owners. But you must go a little deeper than that.

Most pet blogs appeal to a large demographic. You can strip away demographic divisions such as age, gender, and income when you are writing about a general pet topic that many different people will find relevant.

A lot of the content you create will likely appeal to a general audience, so just write in a way you think pet owners would relate to. The kind of pet you are writing about and the purpose of the information you are sharing will just naturally attract the kinds of people who can relate.

I once read somewhere that all of your writing should be on a fifth-grade level. This may not be true for dense research articles, but in the case of a blog, I think it is quite applicable. If a ten-year-old can read and understand what you are talking about, then you can appeal to a wide demographic.

However, maybe your topic in itself appeals to a very particular demographic. A blog about apartment living with a big dog would only appeal to a specific category of people; a lot of people with different living circumstances or small dogs will not find your topic at all relevant.

Therefore, you must always write to this specific category of people. Focus your content on what they would care about. Use language that they can understand and relate to, and share stories about your experiences that they will likely identify with.

Always tailor your writing to your demographic.

- Are they going to be pet lovers looking for something lighthearted and cheerful?
- Are they going to be people suffering from serious pet-related issues, looking for help or grief support?
- Does the topic you are writing about in a particular post fit in with this demographic, or should it get a separate blog with a separate audience of its own?

Ask yourself, "Will this fit in with what my demographic is looking for?" Figure out what your target demographic wants and use that to drive your content.

Information-rich articles supported by scientific research will appeal to those seeking education on pet health or nutrition, step-by-step listicles with pictures will appeal to those looking for instructions, and lighthearted personal stories with a few pictures will appeal to those looking for heartwarming pet stories to brighten their day. Your content must align with your niche, and your niche must align with your target demographic.

You might consider tweaking a blog post to appeal more to your demographic if you see that you are getting little traffic or earning negative comments.

Often, you won't know what people like until you try something out and get feedback. Don't take negative feedback personally; use it constructively and grow from it.

Once, I was very hurt by a comment in which a woman complained that I did not offer much information in a post. Then I realized, "She is just expressing a need for more information. I can add more depth to my posts and thus appeal to more people."

By taking her comment as constructive criticism, I was able to formulate the writing style I use to this day. Blogging is a learning and growth experience for all of us!

You should read some pet blogs to see what they are doing. This can serve as inspiration for your own blog. Call it market research and look into what people want from pet blogs. However, keeping your own voice is essential. Your voice is what makes your blog uniquely yours. Don't just copy what others are doing. Stand out by doing your own thing.

You may find something is trending and you want to hop on the bandwagon. That is always a good short-term strategy which can really work to drive traffic.

However, in time, that topic will no longer be trending. Having a solid niche that will endure through time will ensure loyalty from your readers for years to come. Don't just do what everyone else is doing.

You can stand out and leave your impression on the blogosphere by creating something that will stay relevant.

For instance, writing about feeding your dog grain-free may be a great one-time post that fits in with the big trend on the Internet right now, but offering other content on doggie nutrition will endure long after that fad has passed and pet owners start seeking a different feeding regimen.

CHOOSING YOUR BLOG TITLE

Once you have decided on your niche, you must think of a title that accurately reflects your niche. The title of your blog is so important because it contains keywords relating to your topic, making it possible for people to find it when they Google something. Plus, people are going to click on your blog when they see that the title is relevant to them.

Too many details and unnecessary words in your title can make someone lose interest rapidly. The average attention span of a person racing through a long list of websites on a Google search is about three seconds. This is not much time for someone to process an excessively wordy title.

Short and sweet is the name of the game. Consider these two examples: "rorysblogaboutturtlesandotherthings.com" versus "rorysturtlesandmore.com." Which one of these titles would you be more inclined to click on?

In a copywriting course, you learn to condense long-winded sentences into a few snappy words that sum up the entire message in a neat little package with a bow on top. That's why ads have little sentence fragments that roll off the tongue easily, rather than sentences befitting a dissertation.

The elements of copywriting apply to your blog's title, since the title is essentially selling your blog in a few words. It can be helpful to write a complete, lengthy sentence expressing your blog's purpose. Then pare it down to the few words that really matter. Read them aloud in different ways until you find a pleasing combination that works.

Something fun is always attractive to readers. Say you are writing a dog food review blog. You could title it "feedingdogs.com" or "caninenutrition.com," but that's a bit boring. You will appeal to more people if you came up with something creative and cute, like "feedingfido.com" or "thedoggiebowl.com."

Once you have an idea, go back to the sentence you have pared down to a few words and see if you can replace any common or boring words with more interesting ones. A thesaurus is always a helpful reference.

Remember, pet owners love their pets. They want to read blogs that use fun, affectionate, enthusiastic language to reflect that love. Calling dogs "doggies"—or my favorite, "doggo"—is one way to express the fondness you share with your readers and for the canine species.

Return to your sentence one last time and see if you can replace a word with something a bit more affectionate, silly, or fun. For instance, in my travels I saw a business called "Fish and Phips," and they run a fascinating blog by the same name.

By using the slang word for amphibians, they managed to create a business name and blog title that is far more appealing to amphibian owners.

Plus, "Fish and Phips" rolls off the tongue a bit more pleasingly than the clunky and boring "Fish and Amphibians."

Alliteration and rhyming are both aesthetically and sonically appealing. Creating a title that uses one or both of these elements creates something that people can remember.

This is why you should read your title aloud several times. See if it clicks nicely with your brain, or if it seems awkward and stilted.

Of course, you may not want to use silly or fun words in a blog about a more serious topic. My pet grief support blog addresses a topic that carries deep gravity. I wouldn't want to make light of it, so my title uses serious words that relate directly to my topic.

It all boils down to the niche you are filling. If you are writing about a serious topic, there is still no reason to come up with a name that does not read nicely. You can find new words to replace ones that don't sound so good.

You can trim unnecessary "fat," so to speak, from long-winded titles, too. A serious topic still should not have a boring title.

If you own a business and wish your blog to center around it, then a logical title would be your business name. That way, when people look you up, they will locate your blog. Having your blog on your website (Glossary) is a great way to drive sales. I'll talk about that more in Chapter 8.

When you register your blog, you will have to put in your title (Chapter 3). Condense the title of your blog into all lowercase and follow it with ".com." Should your chosen title be taken, don't try changing it from ".com" to ".org" or ".net." If you do, your title is not unique and may be confused with the other blog site.

THE CRUCIALITY OF SEO

SEO, or search engine optimization, can be the bane of any new blogger's existence because it calls for using a lot of the same words, which can feel tedious. But in time, you will realize how essential it is to ranking higher in searches.

The more you use keywords (Glossary and Chapter 6) for your different articles and the more often you use them within each article, the more likely a search engine will pull up your page to the front when someone searches for a specific thing.

When you Google something, you probably just type in a few words. Then your Google search populates with related sites and you can easily retrieve the information you seek.

You probably don't even bother clicking past the first page, or even the first five or so sites on the list, because what you need is right there on top. That means that the sites on the top of the list get far more traffic than those that hide beyond the first page. You want to be on that first page!

The secret to getting to the top of all of those sites involves inputting the keywords someone is likely to enter in the search bar into your blog. Therefore, you must determine a set of keywords that relate to your blog and your content. You must do this for your page, your title, and each post that you create.

Come up with as many as you can to fit into the most possible searches. You could write a good number of blog posts about frog habitats. Each article would need one specific keyword about frogs, frog habitats, and so on.

Sometimes you may know the specific terms for something, while the average layman does not. A reader might Google "warm rock for lizards" when the technical term is "heating rock." So, you want to optimize your page to respond to common layman's requests, not just the technical name.

Otherwise, fewer people will discover your post on rock heaters. Therefore, do some keyword research and find out what trending keywords are. Great tools for this include Google Keyword Planner, Wordtracker, and Ubersuggest.

Another key part of learning about how to use SEO is researching your competitors. Search for keywords and visit the blogs that pop up on top. How are they different from your blog? Take note of the keywords they use, the way they structure their sites, and the way they use keywords in titles.

Visit their social media pages to glean some clues about how they market themselves and how consumers respond. While you don't want to copy anybody, you can certainly learn a few tips from the pros who already rank highly on search engines.

Research keywords and create a chart with your highest ranking, mid-ranking, and lower ranking keywords. Make sure you add both short-tailed keywords and long-tailed keywords (Glossary). Put this list aside for later.

Once you have your keywords, you need to enter them for your site. On your blog's host, you will have a place where you enter a description of your site. Input your keywords here. Also, if you can, work those keywords into your title.

When you create a post, you will need to enter a meta description.

The meta description tells search engines how to present your page, or in other words, what keyword needs to be entered in the search engine in order to retrieve your page. Always use your keyword, and make it very specific what your post is about. Google and other search engines will then know what to do with it. Don't be shy about telling search engines what to do.

SEO does not necessarily mean that you need to use the same words over and over in your blog post; that is a common misunderstanding that many new bloggers have, and you will get into trouble with the search engines. But do try to use them as much as possible. That way, the bots employed by big search engines will locate these words within your blog when someone types those same words into a search. Then, like magic, your site ranks on top and gets more traffic.

Ensuring that your metadata keyword matches the content of your post will also ensure that your site ranks highly because the search engine will find your site and display it based on the match between someone's search and your meta description.

You might add some additional related keywords that someone is likely to use in a search to your metadata, too, even if you don't use them in the blog post itself.

Once you have figured out your keywords and input them, you can use a variety of tools to ensure that your blog is optimized, or using your keywords in a suitable way. These tools will search your site and make sure that your keywords are used enough. They will also provide useful suggestions for how to improve titles and where to enter meta descriptive data.

Some are plug-ins that you can use from your blog, such as WordPress SEO by Yoast. This is my favorite because Yoast lets you know if you used your keyword appropriately, if your post is easy to read, and gives you suggestions on how to improve your article.

If you use Wix, there is a built-in SEO Optimizer. Others, such as

Google Keyword Planner or Keyword Tool, allow you to search keywords and see how they rank.

I do most of my keyword research myself, but I also use Fiverr (Resources). I have hired various freelancers that have provided very useful lists when I am feeling pressed for time. These lists have been extremely useful and successful for me.

Finally, don't forget to use your keywords on your social media posts. That helps them rank higher in searches, while also communicating what your blog post is about to users. Using them as relevant hashtags (Glossary) can help you accomplish higher rankings on social media, as well. If you are posting ads, be sure to use keywords in them, as well.

SEO is a huge topic, and I can't cover it all in this book. Conducting your own research is essential to being a successful pet blogger with many loyal followers. This is a good introduction on how to use them in your blog. Also, see Chapters 3 and 6 for more extensive information on SEO.

POST REGULARLY

To stay relevant, you must post regularly. Every day may be a bit much to ask of any busy person, but set a schedule for weekly posts. Having a certain day that you publish a new post can appeal to people, since they know when to visit your blog for new content.

You will also find that posting on a certain day allows you to automate emails to people who have signed up for your blog's email list, notifying readers of new content when you post it.

Imagine visiting a blog and finding that the blogger has not posted anything for six months. How likely are you to follow this blog?

You will probably read one or two posts that apply to you and then move on. You assume that this blog is going defunct and nothing new will appear, so you don't bother following or revisiting. You don't want people to treat your blog like this.

Posting regularly helps people see that you are an active member of the little online community you have created, and so they want to join in.

Time moves fast on the Internet. Old posts rapidly get buried by newer posts. Have you ever found a great blog post, forgot to bookmark it, and then failed to ever find it again when you search for it because hundreds of new sites have leapt up higher in the search engine ranking?

This can happen to your blog before you know it. To stay at the top of your SEO ranking, you must keep posting.

Last but certainly not least, not posting regularly will cause a decline in followers, as readers realize you are not offering them anything new. To keep followers, you want to engage your readers with new content.

You also want to offer various ways for readers to follow you so that they know when you post something new. Posting links to new content to your social media feeds and sending emails to people who have signed up for your email list will accomplish this.

There are tools that enable you to automate these social media posts and emails within WordPress and other blogging software.

We all need a vacation, and sometimes unexpected things come up. If something happens and you can't post, notify your followers that you will be taking a brief hiatus but you will be returning.

Provide a date when they can expect new content. Even send everyone on your email list an email notification to ensure they know why they haven't heard from you in a while. That way, you don't lose followers who think you have simply stopped writing.

DARE TO BE DIFFERENT

I cannot stress it enough: The real key to getting followers is appealing to them. And the only way to appeal to people is to have your blog with your own unique spin on your theme.

There are other people in your niche; how do you stand out from them and get people to follow you? The answer is being bold and offering readers something different from what they can get from competitors.

You may even have an idea that allows you to create your own niche that no one has done before; it may not trend, but it is worthwhile to take a risk and try anyway.

You may have many followers who subscribe to other blogs in your niche. You can't expect to have exclusive loyalty with every person who follows your blog.

However, if you can offer readers something that stays with them even as they peruse other blogs of the same nature, you will give them something that makes them stick around and keep reading.

Do something bold and memorable. A certain adorable story, a powerful backstory in your "About Me" section (Chapter 4), an article with some rare information or impactful points that you don't see in your competitors' posts: these are all viable ways to win and maintain loyalty amongst your followers. Even just a really creative title will make you stand out from the competition (Chapter 5).

Be sure to stay true to yourself and you will stand out from competitors regardless, simply because every blogger is different.

If you are a humorous writer, add some humor and jokes to your blog. If you like to muse, ask a question and then invite your readers to chime in on the comments. If you are great at research or if you can offer interesting perspectives on issues, then do that as much as applicable in your blog.

Your readers will fall in love with your voice. They feel that they connect with you in some way. The little glimpses you offer them into your own mind generates a sense of fellowship and a bond that attracts and maintains followers. So be unique to give people a reason to want to read what you have to say.

Your blog is also a community. As you post your thoughts, people respond in comments. If you have guest bloggers or run the blog with other writers, you have even more people joining in the community. By actively engaging with your readers, you create kinship and a sense of personal connection that people like. This makes people feel more loyal to your blog.

You are already part of a community of other pet owners; putting yourself out there with a blog and engaging personally with your readers helps you draw upon those bonds that are already in place.

Dr. Robert Cialdini talks about commitment and consistency in his book *Influence: Science and Practice*. Once someone commits to a brand or cause, they generally stay consistent with it.

You can get people to commit to your blog by giving them things to love about your blog, things that the competitors don't offer in quite the same way, if at all. Unless you give followers a reason to ditch your blog, you will find that they stay loyal. Consistently deliver what you have to offer and you will find fans consistently enjoy your content.

The important thing is to give people something different with your own unique spin on your niche of choice. Then engage with them and build an online community. From there, you will build a loyal following and a robust email list that only grows.

WRAP-UP

You have learned about picking a niche. Your blog needs a definitive purpose. Draw from your inspiration and look to the changes you want to make in the pet world.

Don't pigeonhole yourself with a topic that is too narrow, but don't pick something so broad that your readers won't know what your blog is about.

You have learned how to tie up your purpose in a title that expresses what your blog is about. Your title says who you are. Pick a short and concise one that sums your purpose up neatly. A course in copywriting can be helpful.

Consider this a brief introduction to SEO for your site. Do some research on keywords using handy keyword tools so that you rank higher in searches. That will drive more traffic to your blog.

You don't want to be hiding on some back page of a Google search; your goal is to appear on the first page when your readers search for relevant keywords.

Posting regularly is key. Don't let your blog fall to the wayside. If you are going to be gone for a while, let your readers know.

Finally, find your unique voice. Stand out from the crowd. The only way to attract a readership is to offer them something the competition doesn't. You might fret that you have nothing to offer, but you do with your ideas. No one else has the same ideas as you.

Use the three action steps at the end of this chapter to help you find your niche, choose your name, and figure out your keywords. This will help you plan and organize your blog.

Now, read on to learn more about hosting. This next chapter will show you the secrets to finding a domain name and a place for your blog on the Internet. It really isn't as hard as it seems! I will show you how to use my favorite host and get your blog up and running in no time.

ACTION STEPS

Listed are the steps I covered in this chapter. Use the action steps as a checklist as you proceed with creating your blog. Refer back in this chapter to gain more detail when you are ready for the tasks outlined below.

STEP 1: FIND YOUR NICHE

Look into your heart and locate the one thing you are most passionate about in the pet world. That should be your niche.

On a piece of paper, jot down all of your ideas for blog posts. Narrow them down to a few that fit into the overarching purpose of your blog.

It is also helpful to write down your niche in clear language for future reference. Should you have lots of ideas that don't fit into one niche, you could consider opening more than one blog.

Based on your niche, also figure out what your audience, or demographic, will be. Use this to drive your content and your language. It should even drive your title and your chosen WordPress theme (Chapter 4).

STEP 2: CHOOSE YOUR NAME

On a piece of paper, write down the overall purpose of your blog in a long sentence, using as many words as you want.

Then start to trim unnecessary words until you're down to a nice, short title. Replace boring words with more interesting ones. Think of something snappy and cute. Read your title aloud to see if it sounds good.

STEP 3: FIGURE OUT YOUR KEYWORDS

You will do your SEO optimizing later in the blogging process, but now is a good time to figure out your SEO keywords.

That way, you can easily retrieve them as you write. You want to create a chart with highest ranking, middle ranking, and lowest ranking keywords.

II

SETTING UP YOUR BLOG

3

FINDING A HOME FOR YOUR BLOG

The magic thing about home is that it feels good to leave, and it feels even better to come back. — Wendy Wunder

You have drummed up your courage, tapped into your inspiration, conceived the topic of your blog, picked a great title, determined some keywords, and possibly even created some content. But what do you do with it? Well, now it's time to go public!

To launch your blog, you first must find a host. A host is essentially the home wherein your blog dwells on the Internet. Hosting servers are companies that keep your blog running and maintain your domain name for varying fees.

There are many, many hosts out there, but the best one, in my opinion, is SiteGround (Resources). With their amazing customer service, I have no complaints. Another popular one is BlueHost, though I did not have the best experiences with them.

You should avoid GoDaddy since you are an animal lover; the CEO is a trophy hunter who proudly displays his kills on the Internet.

Some people may think of hosting as the hard part. I can't promise you it will be easy because everyone has a different skill set when it comes to technology. But if you are adventurous, I urge you to try.

I will show you how to basically use SiteGround. If you want more detailed instructions, please go to their website and contact customer care, as they are extremely helpful. I will also briefly talk about two free server options, as well.

If you choose a different hosting service, it should be self-explanatory if you are computer savvy. If you are not so tech savvy, watch a YouTube tutorial on how to use the service. You will be amazed at the number of instructional posts you can find on YouTube.

STEP 1: GET READY FOR SITEGROUND

Are you ready to take the plunge into your first blog? Okay, here we go!

Visit SiteGround and pick a plan. Currently, there are three plans.

The first (and cheapest) is called StartUp. It offers you one site, ten gigabytes of storage, and ten thousand monthly visits. It comes with all of the features you need for a basic blog, including: free SSL certificates, unmetered traffic, daily backup, and 24/7 support.

The thirty-day money back guarantee is also great, in case you don't like SiteGround and want to move hosts. This plan might be a great option if you are intending on starting only one blog. You can always start with this and then upgrade later on if you need more storage, more visits, or more sites.

However, I wanted a little more wiggle room to grow as a blogger, plus I have three websites, so I went with the middle option.

This is called GrowBig, and it is tailored to those who want to grow on the web. It offers multiple websites, twenty thousand visits per month, and twenty gigabytes of storage.

This should be more than enough for your needs as a blogger starting out. You will get the room to grow that you need, and you will also have plenty of visits and storage. As you get started, you won't have that many visits.

Don't get discouraged about this, as that will change if you put in the work!, and twenty thousand is more than enough when you are starting out. Again, you can always upgrade if you need.

The main thing I like about this middle plan is that it boasts premium features for just a few dollars more than the StartUp plan.

Premium features include site transfer, which is great if you already have a site on a different server. You get priority technical support, so your emails will be answered first. There is SuperCacher, which makes your site run faster. And you get free backup restores. That is a great deal and makes the few dollars extra worth it!

There is still another tier. GoGeek is "for the real web geeks." This is the one for you if you are looking to start several sites with advanced features. You get thirty gigabytes of storage, a hundred thousand monthly visits, and essential, premium, *and* "geeky advanced" features.

What are these "geeky advanced" features? You get fewer accounts on the server, which can make your sites run and load faster. You get WordPress and Joomla! staging; in other words, you get dummy sites where you can test out new features before you actually publish them into your real site.

You also get PCI-compliant servers, which basically means that you can safely accept payments from users of your site as a merchant. You get a one-click git repo creation, or basically a storage cache of files that change over time called a "repository."

Finally, you get free backups. All of these features are necessary to host a merchant site or a constantly evolving site, but they are not so necessary for the average blogger. You may not need this plan, depending on your niche.

I am not going to talk about fees in this book, simply because fees change and you may find different rates in the future. However, these plans go up by a few dollars for each tier.

You essentially get what you pay for. I think the lowest tier, or the cheapest plan, is sufficient; the middle plan is ideal; and the top one is probably more than you need.

STEP 2: REGISTER YOUR DOMAIN

Once you pick your plan, click or tap on the big "Order Now" button. This takes you to a page asking you to register your domain. You can choose "register a new domain" if you don't already have a blog. Otherwise, click "I already have a domain." Then enter your domain name in the bar underneath your selection.

Click "Proceed" and you are taken to a page that asks you to review and complete your submission. This is where you get to enter your email, your chosen password, your address, and your payment information.

You also get to select the time duration in which you will use the service. I just left it at "twelve months," the default option.

You can renew within a year easily. SiteGround will automatically notify you as soon as your expiration date draws near.

Now, let's say you enter your domain name, and the site says that this name is not available for registration. In Chapter 2, I discussed tweaking your domain name. If someone already has your domain name registered, you can add or take away little words. But I don't suggest changing the .com to .org or .net or .info, as this is not considered a unique domain name.

Your blog name is part of who you are, and it speaks to your readers, so having a name too similar to another site is a bad idea. It is best to find something unique. Someone can easily get confused if your site is funwithfido.net and someone else already has funwithfido.com.

STEP 3: TRANSFER A DOMAIN

In a different direction, if you already have a domain name, you need to transfer it. SiteGround handles the transfer so you don't have to communicate with your old host and your new one at the same time.

It is very easy. Simply go to your user area and tap the green "Get" button next to "Domain Transfer."

Next, you're going to see a "Product Information" box, where you can type your domain name in the box. The system will automatically detect and notify you of the status of your domain and whether or not you can transfer it.

The most common issue you may find here is that your domain is locked in its server. You have to go into your old host and unlock the domain from your control panel.

To find out how to do this, look at tutorials for unlocking within your specific host server. Usually, it's pretty easy and straightforward.

Your domain also has to be active, meaning that it is published and running on the old host. It has to have been published and active for more than sixty days, and it can't be less than fifteen days from expiring on your old server.

Furthermore, you must obtain your authorization code, or your EPP code, from your old server in order to prove ownership and authorize the transfer. You can find your EPP by going into your old server and looking it up.

If you have met all of the requirements, then the transfer will be straightforward. SiteGround will tell you so and load a box where you enter your EPP code. Once you enter the code, SiteGround will begin the transfer.

Sit back and enjoy some tea while you wait. You might expect an email from your old server, asking for you to confirm the transfer. Be sure to confirm it or the transfer won't take place.

SiteGround will send you an email welcoming you when the transfer is completed. You're in!

STEP 4: FILL IN YOUR WHOIS INFORMATION

WHOIS (Glossary) is the information about you and how to contact you. You must keep it accurate and up to date for your site to work properly. SiteGround may suspect your site if your information falls out of date.

First, go to your user area. From here, go to the domain you want to edit (This is very easy if you have only one domain.) and click "Manage" to the right. A page full of your information then pops up. Edit the information that needs to be updated.

You can also ask your former server to send that information through your EPP code if you have transferred a domain.

Now that you have done that, you should look into the SiteGround privacy tool. For most sites on SiteGround, you have to order this additionally. This tool masks all of your information and enters SiteGround's information instead so that hackers won't be able to retrieve your address or email. Your email won't get harvested and added to millions of spam lists.

To add this privacy tool, go to your user area again, find your domain, and click on "Add ID Protect," which is on your far right.

STEP 5: SET UP YOUR SITE

Now, here's the fun part. You will be building your site using WordPress, which I cover in more detail in the next chapter. Then you must upload it to SiteGround using a handy wizard within the server.

Enter your user area. A wizard will pop up, inviting you to start a new website, transfer a website, or "Don't need help now." Click on starting a new website if you haven't started your own yet.

Then you will see a list of website-building software. You can select any one you would like, but I use and recommend WordPress. It should be your first option. Joomla! is another popular one.

Select the software you want and hit "Confirm" at the bottom. It will start setting up your new software. Now you can use it right away. You can also select "I do not want to set up now. Remind me next time I log in."

If you select that option, SiteGround will pause the setup and save it for up to thirty days. You can start the setup whenever you are ready by simply logging in.

If this doesn't work for you for some reason, you can contact SiteGround through their support. Request help downloading the software of your choice. You will encounter a list of common support topics. Select "Install WordPress" or any other option that applies to you.

The support team will happily assist you. I have had excellent experiences using the SiteGround support, which is why I favor it as a host server over others.

Now, if you have already created a website, don't select "Start a new website." Click on "Transfer a website" instead. Then hit "Confirm." The SiteGround support team will then handle the transfer for you so you don't have to build a whole new site.

The best part of this is that you can order a site transfer for a small fee if you have the StartUp plan, but you get one free transfer with your GrowBig plan.

The team can transfer every part of your old website if you were operating it on cPanel (see Glossary), from email accounts to configurations. Otherwise, the team can only copy over most elements of your old site, minus your email accounts and configurations.

It is also possible to transfer your site manually, though it is more difficult and time-consuming. You need to use a file transfer protocol between your previous host and SiteGround. Then you need to move your database over.

Finally, you need to reconfigure your whole application. I think it is far better to just let SiteGround do all of that for you!

STEP 6: CREATE EMAIL ACCOUNTS

For numerous reasons, you don't want your personal email receiving all correspondence from your blog. First, it looks more professional to have a contact email that uses your blog's name, such as susan@susanspetblog.com.

Second, you can stop email harvesting and hacking with this extra security measure, and you can block spam using SiteGround's built-in spam filter. Finally, you can keep everything organized nicely.

Your SiteGround plan (regardless of which one you choose) comes with unlimited free email accounts. The different plans do put limits on how much space you get with your email account, however. Be mindful of that, and be sure to clean out old emails to conserve space.

Visit your user area. Click on "My Accounts" and then "Go to cPanel" and "Mail section." There, you should find an email icon and the name "Email Accounts." Click on that. Some text fields should pop up, asking for your email name, your password, and your chosen mailbox quota.

The mailbox quota is just how much space you want to dedicate to your email storage. The quota can't exceed the space you are allotted with your plan. StartUp is 2000 MB, GrowBig is 4000 MB, and GoGeek is 6000 MB. To simplify things, I just specified the limit for my plan, 4000 MB, and left it at that.

After you have filled everything in, hit "Create Accounts." Your email account is instantly generated. Now you can get correspondence through your blog!

It is critical to install the email to your phone and computer so that you can stay on top of your emails. Or you can direct your business email to your personal email using the prompts in SiteGround.

If you want to install the email to your phone and computer, enter your email account on your phone and select "Add Account." Then configure the account using the requested information.

On your computer, you can do the same and configure your account with your desktop email application. That way, you can get notified of emails whenever and wherever you are away from your desk.

STEP 7: SET UP YOUR SSL CERTIFICATE

Your SSL certificate is your ticket to safety on the Internet. It is a bit of data that locks your site to an https encryption.

This keeps your site secure and enables people to navigate your site without their browsers blocking it due to security risks. A bad SSL configuration will make most browsers block your site, simply because your site has "holes" that allows viruses to infect others and hackers to retrieve information.

First, go to your user area and click on "cPanel." Hit the "Security" tab and then "Let's Encrypt." This brings up a list of your domains on SiteGround. Select the one you are working with and hit the "Install" button at the very bottom of the page. This installs encryption and keeps your site safe.

It also automatically renews every three months, so you don't have to remember to do so yourself. The best part is that it is free.

Wildcard is another encryption solution to your site. It is ideal if you have subdomains. Or you can try Extended Validation SSL if you are running a site that needs top-level encryption for processing cards and storing user information. Both of these are paid.

You can also enter SSL certificates yourself if you obtain them through other means. Go to "cPanel" and then select "Security" and find the tab with "SSL/TLS Manager." You will find a variety of settings here.

For further security, you need to configure your SSL certificate to work on every part of your site. Once again, go to your user area and select "cPanel." Then hit "Let's Encrypt" and peruse the "Action" drop-down menu. Tap on "HTTPS Settings." A new window pops up, asking if you want to allow redirections and other such things. Be sure to toggle each option on.

You can also install the SG Optimizer plug-in within WordPress. This accomplishes the same thing within your site. It is all easy enough, even if you don't understand all of the computer jargon.

STEP 8: LEARN THE SITEGROUND TOOLS

The tools within SiteGround help you master your site and offer a wide range of useful features. Getting to know them is imperative to operating your site. Fortunately, most of the tools are very intuitive. SiteGround offers tutorials on each one.

Support through SiteGround is also very helpful in all situations. We all know how fickle technology and software can be. You are likely to run into some sort of problem. Support is always available, 24/7/365, and they truly care. You can get answers to your questions and help solving issues within your site very quickly.

FREE OPTIONS

If you are not interested in paying for your domain, you can explore certain free options. These options offer you a basic website and a domain name that combines your blog's name with the server's name.

For instance, your free domain would be something like wendysblog.wix.com. This does not look as professional or as polished as having your own domain, but if you want to save money, it is a great option.

Probably the best free host would be Wix. Visit wix.com and create an account. Start a site and design it using the Wix in-site tools. Once your site is completed to your liking, you can publish it and enter your domain name. For a fee, you can upgrade to your own domain name, as well.

Other free options include weebly.com and webs.com. These sites work just like Wix. They have fewer design options in the site, however.

CONGRATULATIONS!

Believe it or not, you are now the official owner of a real blog. You are no longer fantasizing about starting a blog someday; you have actually started one! With your own site, you have taken the second huge step toward success as a pet blogger.

It can only get better from here. You have done the first hard part, navigating the technical part of launching a website. Now you have just one more technical part, where you create your blog on WordPress, and then you are ready to launch your blog.

After the next step, you will have an operational blog on the Internet, and you can start creating your online community and posting content from your heart. You did it!

I think some congratulations are in order. Take yourself out and celebrate! You are now on your way to becoming a blogger!

WRAP-UP

You have learned all about starting up on SiteGround. You have learned how to pick a plan, register your domain, transfer your site, start your site with WordPress, verify encryption, and create email accounts.

It is all straightforward, even if you are not a computer whiz, because

SiteGround automates everything for you, and their customer service is excellent.

With your site up and running, it is time to create your actual content. You will do this using WordPress, or any other software of your choice. Because WordPress is the most common and the most popular (for good reason), I will only cover using WordPress in the following chapter.

If you pick a different software, look up tutorials on how to use it. SiteGround offers you the freedom to download different software for this purpose.

It is time to pat yourself on the back. Having completed these steps, you officially own your very own blog. You have etched out your little personal space in the blogosphere, and you have taken one more step than most people, who only dream of starting a blog but never take the initiative to actually start one.

You may have noticed this chapter consisted of action steps, but I have still outlined the steps for you to use as a checklist to get your site up and running without missing anything.

The fun part has just begun! Are you ready to create the content that makes your blog its own beautiful creation? Then read on!

ACTION STEPS

> Listed are the steps I covered in this chapter. Use the action steps as a checklist as you proceed with creating your blog. Refer back in this chapter to gain more detail when you are ready for the tasks outlined below.

Step 1: Sign Up With Siteground (or another host)

Step 2: Register Your Domain

Step 3: Fill in WHOIS Information

Step 4: Set Up Your Site With Wordpress (or another platform)

Step 5: Create Your Email Accounts

Step 6: Set Up Your SSL Certificate

Step 7: Learn the SiteGround Tools

4

WORDPRESS BOOTCAMP

Your limitation—it's only your imagination. — Anonymous

In the last chapter, you learned about setting up your site with SiteGround. But now you need to actually create your site. You will do this using the WordPress software application within SiteGround.

Here's a little boot camp to get you up and running with WordPress. Keep in mind, I couldn't possibly cover all the aspects of using WordPress in this book, but I will point you in the right direction to get further help.

SET UP WORDPRESS

To get WordPress, access your user area on your SiteGround account and find your accounts. Locate the domain you are customizing with WordPress. Hit the "Manage Account" button on the far right next to your domain name. Now you'll see a few tabs on top. Select the orange one that says, "Go to cPanel."

A pop-up will appear asking if you're sure. Select "Access cPanel Securely." A page appears with a lot of options. At the bottom, there should be a section called "Autoinstallers." You'll see the WordPress icon here. Click on that.

Another pop-up will appear. At the bottom left-hand corner, there is a button that says, "Install Now." Select that. Now you come to a software setup page. On the right-hand side, there is a dropdown menu. Select the "HTTP" option with your mouse and then enter your domain name in the blank. If you have your SSL certificate set up, select the "HTTPS" option.

You will also see a blank for "In Directory." Leave this part blank.

Now, on this same exact page, you'll see a place asking for your site name and your site description. This is where that handy SEO introduction in Chapter 2 comes into play.

You should already have your title picked out and your site description. Enter them in the appropriate slots.

Don't just enter something like "my site" in the title slot. Enter your actual blog name, as this will recall your blog in searches. Under description, use tons of keywords as you fill out a sentence that perfectly describes your blog's purpose.

Spare no details. A long description that hits lots of keywords is better than something short that maybe hits one possible keyword.

Finally, enter your username and your password. You can use your personal email or your SiteGround email. I use my SiteGround email for this part. Pick a strong password and write it down. You will need it every time you access WordPress to write a post. Choose your language from the dropdown menu. Hit "Complete."

SiteGround should generate a success page. It will say, "Congratulations, the software was installed successfully." This page has a key piece of information: your site URL. It will be your domain name plus "/wp-admin/." Definitely save this URL!

Now copy and paste this URL into your browser. It will take you to a WordPress page where you can enter your username and password. Log in, and you're ready to start creating your masterpiece.

GET FAMILIAR WITH WORDPRESS

WordPress is relatively easy to use. Once you become familiar with it, you will have very few problems with it. However, it involves a learning curve. Before you even start writing posts, you should take some time to play around with WordPress and find out how to use it.

When you first enter your WordPress, you will be met by a stark white page. On the right-hand side, you will see a search bar, a section for posts, and a section for comments. On the left-hand side, you will see a blank post. "Welcome to WordPress. This is your first post. Edit or delete it, then start writing!"

Start by visiting your dashboard. This is where you control every part of your blog. Get familiar with the buttons and where they go. You'll see a list of options on the left of your page, posts, media, pages, comments, and appearance.

ADD AVADA THEME

Yay! This is where you get to find yourself and express yourself through your blog. I found customizing my site's appearance to be my favorite part of the whole process. It is super fun.

I love the Avada theme. Super easy. It is the best-selling WordPress theme because it makes everything easy for the user. You don't need to learn how to code, as Avada does it for you. It generates a powerful and customizable theme that allows you to design your site as you see fit.

I'm going to talk about Avada here, but if you want to install your own theme, you can shop for themes on WordPress. With over six thousand themes on WordPress, you are sure to find something you like. Many are free, though some cost money.

To get them, go to "Appearance" on your dashboard and then click on "Add New" and click on themes. You can hover your mouse over the theme you like to see two buttons, "Preview" and "Install." Preview everything to ensure you like it.

Remember, you can customize most things within a theme, such as your colors or your title fonts. The overall layout will primarily stay the same based on the theme. When you find a theme you love, click on the "Install" button.

HOW TO INSTALL AVADA

You can install Avada from within your WordPress dashboard. I will cover how you can get started, but I recommend the website Avadaphile.com, where you can find helpful and detailed tutorials.

First, you must get Avada. There is a beginner package that you can download. Be sure to save the downloaded files into your "Downloads" or somewhere else so that it is easy to find. You'll need to be able to retrieve the downloaded files for your WordPress upload.

Second, go to "Appearance." Click on "Add New" and then the "Upload Theme" button. Click on "Choose File." Find your theme file and click on it. It will then upload.

If you are uploading the full package, you first have to right click on the file in your computer and unzip it. It will display several files. Click on the second one in the list when you go to upload it through WordPress.

Now go back to your themes page on your WordPress dashboard. Find the theme and click "Activate." This part is essential or your theme won't run!

Once you activate it, you will be redirected to a welcome page. You can install all of the necessary plug-ins from within Avada and begin customizing your site from here.

Some people get an error. This is because your host has placed a limit on the files you can upload and won't accept your theme. That's when you have to use FTP to upload Avada to WordPress. Let's go over that.

You should use a service like FileZilla for this. Log in to your server installation. Now unzip your Avada file and use the second one to upload it to the *wp-content > themes* folder on the server.

That's it! All you have to do is go into your WordPress themes and click the "Activate" button for the Avada theme. It should already be sitting there in your themes, waiting to be activated. If it isn't, try refreshing the page.

A FEW TIPS FOR YOUR SITE'S APPEARANCE

Strive to make your site simple and clean. No one is going to have the patience to read a convoluted blog with tons of links everywhere and no clear organization.

Using Avada, display all of your pages in a menu bar, organize your content into neat individual containers, and provide everything in a layout that trains the eye on one thing at a time.

Colors should not be distracting, and you should not pick font colors that are hard to read against the background. Your pictures should not take away from the fonts, either.

Another thing that is crucial is making your site responsive. With more and more people using their phones to search the Internet every day, you want your blog to be adaptable to mobile viewing. People will lose interest in your site if they can't load it on any device. Simple and responsive themes are critical in this era.

Furthermore, your blog should be compatible with different browsers, or at least the main ones (Google Chrome, Firefox, Internet Explorer, and Safari). Some themes display perfectly on Firefox but break on Chrome. Therefore, you lose every single person who uses Chrome, which represents a significant number of potential followers.

Most themes will say that they have been tested on different browsers, but you can also run the theme yourself by installing it and then checking out your domain from different browsers. A theme that runs smoothly and quickly on each browser is ideal.

Make sure your blog's appearance is congruent with your blog's purpose. A fun blog about how to care for a dog would feature light-hearted images of dogs, bright colors, and fun language.

A blog about pet grief would be more serious, perhaps with blue or gray colors. It would be odd to have a sad theme and serious language in a blog that is supposed to make people feel happy, or vice versa.

Really think about your niche and your demographic to find the best theme. Realize that you can customize colors and fonts and language, but the overall layout will stay the same.

Visit Pinterest and type in your keywords. See what comes up. This can give you some great ideas for how to customize your blog once you register it. You can also visit pixabay.com for free images that appear professional and high quality (Resources).

USING AVADA

Once you have activated Avada, you can enter it to build your site. You can easily create pages, insert headings, and add pictures and portfolios.

You can also avoid using extra WordPress plug-ins, which can majorly slow down your site, by using the ones inside the theme. Furthermore, there are free demos that show you how to use the theme, or you can go to Avadaphile.com (Resources) for excellent tutorials.

CREATE ESSENTIAL PAGES

Posts are different from pages. Posts are your blog articles, and a page is a separate part of your blog. You will want to create pages for different things within the blog. Here are a few pages you must have:

- Author bio
- Contact form
- Blog
- Products or services, if applicable

- Information page about a cause you are supporting, if applicable.

STEPS TO CREATE A PAGE ON YOUR BLOG:

Step 1: Go to the "Pages" tab in WordPress and click "Add New."

Step 2: Title your page in the "Title" field on top.

This is not where you have to get fancy. You can make the title of the page clear and concise. "Contact Me" for a contact page, "About Me" for an author bio page, and so on is sufficient.

Once you title the page, the permalink will appear, generated by the title you entered. You can always edit this from your editor if you need.

Usually, you can just leave this alone. You would only want to edit it if you wanted to make it more keyword-rich or specific.

Step 3: Change the parent settings and template from your "Page Attributes" box.

This is where you set up everything that governs how your page looks.

Page templates help you set up your pages as you want them. You can adjust width to affect the display. You should still find plenty that are both responsive and possible to use on many different browsers.

Parent settings help you create a "Side Navigation" page. This allows you to put a lot of content on one page. It is essential for online stores, product reviews, and blog pages.

All you have to do is go to your "Page Attributes" box and select "Side Navigation" page under templates. Add all of your pages to it.

They will be set up alphabetically in the side menu bar, but you can reorder them by inserting a new order in the "Order" field. Then select if the sidebar will be on the right or left. Publish each page and you are done!

Step 4: Add content to your page.

In the editor part of the page, you can enter images and text. Design the page you want. Use the settings on the right side to change fonts, sizes, colors, and layout.

You can even upload images to rest behind your text. Fusion Builder using the Avada theme helps you add different things you may need to your page, as well.

Containers are a convenient way to organize things on your blog. If you are writing a column, don't just make columns in your editor. Use a column container from Avada.

Go to "Builder Containers" and pick one appropriate for your layout on a particular part of your page. Then customize the settings to make it look just the way you want.

When you are finished with your page design, be sure to click the blue "Publish" button on the top of the page. This makes your page public. But it may or may not add the page to your navigation menu.

You must ensure the page is added to this menu to make it easy for site visitors to find it. Go to your home page and ensure that your page is there. If it isn't, a second step is necessary.

Click on "Appearance" on your left menu bar, and then click on "Menus." Your menu should be there by default. If you don't see one, you will have to add one. You can select a menu style from here.

Next to this on your left sidebar, you will see a "Pages" list. Click the box beside the pages you want on your menu. Ideally, all of your pages should be on your menu, unless there's a page you haven't finished creating yet. Then hit the blue "Save Menu" button on the bottom right-hand side and you are done!

To make the blog a cohesive whole that users can easily navigate, I recommend adding as many internal links (Glossary) as you can. That way, a person doesn't have to scour your site to find something you are talking about. They can simply click on your easy-to-read links and go directly to the desired content.

For example: Say you reference a previous blog entry in a post. Don't make a reader go through all of your previous posts to find the entry. Instead, link to it.

Another example for an internal link is when you invite people to contact you in a post. Don't make them skip over to your "Contact Me" page. Offer a link to your "Contact Me" page or a clickable button that says, "Contact Me!" that leads them to the contact page or pulls up a contact form.

To internal link, all you have to do is highlight the text you want to turn into a link with your mouse and then hit the link button at the top of your editor. The link button looks like two chain links hooked together.

A small window will open up asking for the link. Copy and paste the link. This could be a link to an outside webpage or to one of your pages. Just copy and paste the permalink from your other page here if you are linking within your site.

Buttons are great to add. They are clear and grab readers' attention. Plus, they look attractive. Avada has a variety of buttons you can choose from to direct readers where they may want to go.

Large, colorful buttons that clearly say what you want the reader to do are great. "Click to Follow Me on Social Media!" is an example.

Step 5: Set Your Theme Fusion settings.

In your "Fusion Page Options" box, you will see various settings. Use these to customize your page. Theme Fusion is where the magic happens. You can adjust SEO, responsiveness, your logo, your footer and header, your typography, your background, etc. These settings are all located in logical tabs so that you can easily locate them. Be sure to mess with these settings to make your page awesome!

You can also use these settings to add the plug-ins that you would normally get through WordPress. For instance, there is a "WooCommerce" plug-in that lets you set up an online store. There is a portfolio option to display your work, such as pet photography or pictures of your grooming.

ABOUT THE AUTHOR

Using the instructions above, create a page dedicated solely to you. Call this page something like "Meet the Author" or "About Me." This page is going to be your autobiography.

It should show the world who you are with a few sentences and a picture or two. If you are on a team of writers, you might consider a page for each contributor, or a page featuring a list of the contributors and their names, short bios, and pictures. Everyone who writes on this blog needs a bio.

The reason for this is simple. Since your blog is basically selling your voice and your opinions, you want to show readers who you are. You can connect with readers on a more personal level by featuring a picture of your face and a bio highlighting who you are. Prove to them that you are a real person.

For the photo, be sure to include one that is both flattering and appropriate. A picture of your face, or a picture of you with your pets, is ideal here.

The picture needs to show your face clearly. Don't hide it behind hair, hats, sunglasses, or even your pet. Gaze directly at the camera with a warm, inviting smile. Be sure to have lighting behind you, or be in a well-lit area, to make the picture clear.

Don't stand before a cluttered background, such as a busy intersection or a wall painted violent orange, as the background can distract viewers from what is important, your face.

A full body shot is probably not necessary here. Focus on above the shoulders. However, if you want to upload a picture of your full body while you are playing with your pets toward the bottom of your page, that is fine.

Try to feature your pet in the photo for obvious reasons. You might be holding her or standing next to her at a dog show. You might be engaged in an activity with her. Say you are writing a blog on agility for dogs.

A logical good picture would be one of you with your agility dog holding a trophy or one of you with your dog on an agility course.

On the other hand, if you are writing a blog about spiders, you might want to pose with your tarantula and a big smile. Make the photo express who you are and what your blog is about.

Since you are running a pet blog, you should focus a lot on your experience with pets and the pets you own in your bio. Include some pictures of them. If you run a business, or used to run a pet business, be sure to mention that.

Your goal is to establish yourself as an authority on the topic you are writing about. Your experience and your love for pets will prove that you know what you're talking about.

No one is going to read a blog about fish from some guy who has never owned fish; however, they will eagerly pay rapt attention to a blog written by an aquarium owner or someone who has kept saltwater fish for fifteen years.

Think of something else unique about yourself. If you lived in Paris for five years, that is maybe worth mentioning. Mention some of your hobbies and your major accomplishments. While the main focus of your bio should be on your relevant experience with pets and your love for them, you can veer off that topic to give people a more well-rounded glimpse of who you are.

People tend to connect on similarities. Therefore, you want to find things in common with your readers. You will attract and maintain followers based on these common points of interest. Mentioning things you are into or have done can make people identify with you more readily.

CASE STUDY

I have the pleasure of knowing an excellent resource and expert on spiders, Amanda. Amanda was an entomology major who specialized in identifying spiders and advocating for their preservation in ecosystems.

She is a huge contributor on a local Facebook site, where people post photos of spiders they find in their homes to learn what species the spiders are and whether or not they are venomous.

When Amanda started a blog on spiders, she completely omitted a bio. I advised her to create one, so she wrote a sentence about her age and her love of spiders. "That's good," I told her, "but what about your degree? What about all of your experience with identifying spiders and your conservation work?"

Amanda then constructed a wonderful bio, in which she discussed her authority on the subject. She established that she was an expert that people could trust based on her educational background and many years of experience working with spiders.

That bio helped readers trust her words, and it made people want to follow her for accurate information on spiders and their care.

ADD YOUR CONTENT

Go to your dashboard. Click on "Posts" and then select "Add New." A blank post page appears, where you can enter your content. This page is called the "editor" hereafter.

Now, bad things happen all of the time. I'm talking about slow Internet, hard drive crashes, and the like. That's why I like to create my blog posts in a Microsoft Word document that is automatically set to upload to OneDrive.

That way, I can work offline anywhere and my work is backed up when I'm online to protect against computer malfunctions, the bane of any writer. I can also sync Word across many devices so that I can add ideas to my post when I'm on the go or on a different computer. Then, I copy and paste these posts into my WordPress "Add New."

When you make a post, you must always title it. Your title can be long or short, but it needs to state your point. Have your main keyword in it. The top of the editor will feature a bar that says, "Title." Type your title here.

On the right column, scroll down to "Featured Image." This is the thumbnail that goes with your blog post. It will display on your blog and on searches.

You want to use at least one image per blog; the more the merrier! You should always select a relevant featured image, as well. Stock images work wonders, so familiarize yourself with "Librestock," "Pixabay," and other stock image sites that offer free high-quality images (Resources).

Next, scroll down to "Yoast SEO," which I recommended installing in Chapter 2. Fill in your "Focus Keyword" and "Snippet Preview." Your SEO title should contain the title of your post, which includes the keyword and your name and title.

HERE IS AN EXAMPLE OF MINE:

How to Start a Pet Blog | Wendy Van de Poll, Author, Writing Coach

Next, check your slug, which is your post title with dashes: *how-to-start-a-pet-blog*. WordPress will automate this for you based on your article's name, just double-check to see that everything matches up.

Your last step is customizing your "Meta Description." This box must be filled out if you want to rate well on Google. It contains a brief description about your article. You don't get that many words, so make sure you use your keywords and a blurb that entices your reader.

When you are finished writing, set your categories and tags. Go ahead and hit "Publish" at the top of the editor. Once published, you'll be taken to your "Posts" page where you can see your post. Here, you can edit categories and tags.

Keep in mind these are the basics to setting up your first blog. There are many other options you can enhance, but that would take an entire book on the subject. My goal is to get you started right away with the basic information you need. It will be up to you to go further with learning about SEO, etc.

CATEGORIES VERSUS TAGS

With your first post written, you now must sort it into a category and tag it. This part allows for SEO optimization, which makes your site more discoverable by search engines.

The category is the basic and broad grouping that your posts fits into. If you are writing about grooming a dog, you can put it into the category "pets." WordPress has a list of common categories that you must select from a dropdown menu.

You want to pick one or two categories that you generally write in.

Sort posts into these categories. Don't have thirty possible categories for your blog and only have one post in each.

Each post should fit into only one category. A good idea is to start with an umbrella category that applies to your niche. Pets or dogs are good ones, for instance.

Now that you have your category, sort your posts into subcategories under that. If you have a lot of posts dedicated to "grooming" and a lot dedicated to "feeding," these could be your subcategories. Some people choose to forego subcategories and simply add tags, however. It is up to you.

Tags use specific details from your post and convert them into keywords. You want to use as many tags as possible. If you are writing about dog grooming, you want to add tags like dog shampoo, canine shampoo, shampoo safe for pets, pet shampoo, and bathing dogs.

These are just examples, but they illustrate how you should identify and list as many possible tags as you can think of. That way, search engines locate your site more often as people enter different search terms.

Everybody is different, and they will enter different terms, but some are more common than others. That's why researching keywords is critical.

SEO THE HECK OUT OF EACH PAGE AND POST

As you already know, SEO is your leg up as a blogger. Not using or understanding SEO can be the death of a blog because you're not able to place your blog in front of people who will read it. You must use SEO in every part of your blog to rank higher in searches and reach more people.

When you create a page, make sure its slug is the primary keyword. Also, be sure to use lots of keywords in your meta description, including the primary.

Whenever you create a post, be sure to add tons of tags. Also, use specify common keywords that relate to your post's topic and repeat them throughout the post, as well as in titles. This will make your post appear in searches.

As more people visit particular posts, they will also feel inclined to check out the rest of your blog and possibly sign up for your email list. I will cover that more in Chapters 7 and 8.

For now, think of every visitor as a potential lead or customer, and strategize how to get them to come back. I will show you how later, but as long as you have this mentality, you will hopefully be on your way to making money with your blog.

Don't let SEO blind you. Some bloggers make their blogs all about SEO and forget to focus on the number one priority: the readers. SEO is important, but if using keywords makes your blog read in a funky way that isn't appealing, then don't use it.

You want your blog to read smoothly. You want it to be a good experience for your readers. Cater to them more than the SEO-feeding search bots.

A balance of SEO and great language written to your readers is an ideal way to keep a popular, high-ranking blog. The plug-in "Yoast" is an excellent tool to keep your SEO in line.

WRAP-UP

In this chapter, you learned about WordPress and the Avada theme. From setting it up to creating pages and tagging posts, you know the basics of WordPress now. With time, you will learn and become comfortable using this software.

Pages, plug-ins, and posts. You don't need to know code to create and use them. WordPress and Avada does it all for you.

From within your WordPress menu, you can create an amazing blog that is both visually appealing to visitors and convenient to navigate with a menu and cross-links or buttons. Certain plug-ins will make your site interactive, as well.

Keep it clean with what you need. When running a blog, the adage, "Less is more," is always applicable!

Like the previous chapter, I have listed these action steps as a reminder for you as you navigate WordPress."

Now, I think it may be time for you to go have a spa day or enjoy some time with friends or something else you enjoy. You deserve to reward yourself. The "hard part" is now over. You own and run a blog that looks and runs the way you want. You are a winner!

Ready to start actually blogging? Then read on for ideas and tips on how to make enlightening blog posts that keep your readers coming back for more in the next chapter.

ACTION STEPS

> Listed are the steps I covered in this chapter. Use the action steps as a checklist as you proceed with creating your blog. Refer back in this chapter to gain more detail when you are ready for the tasks outlined below.

Step 1: Install WordPress through SiteGround. This part is really easy.

Step 2: Install the Avada theme. You can do this separately and then upload it to your WordPress site.

Step 3: Create pages. Definitely feature an "About the Author" page. Also, feature a shop if you are selling something. Feature a blog page for your blog content.

Step 4: Add your content. Don't let SEO blind you.

5

CREATING WINNING CONTENT

Believe in yourself. You are braver than you think, more talented than you know, and capable of more than you imagine. — Roy T. Bennett

Your site is up and running. You have designed your pages and selected a great theme. Everything looks great. Now what?

Now it's time to publish that content that makes your blog!

Blogs run on the content that they generate. If you are a blogger, then your content comes from the meaningful ideas, suggestions, and stories that you give other people.

Whether your blog is based on providing helpful tips or offering unbiased product reviews, you must put out content to bring in the followers and money.

An empty blog won't get many followers. A blog populated with lots of posts made on a schedule is going to be more successful. That means that you must post, and you must post often.

I will share later in this chapter what tools I use to create well-written articles. For now, I want to concentrate on your awesome ideas for articles, as well as suggestions to make your blogging efforts successful.

LOGO

Your logo is part of your brand. It represents you and makes you easy to recognize. A creative yet effective logo is imperative to your brand. Before you start posting content, be sure to create one.

I recommend PicMonkey. This platform lets you create a free logo that fits your brand. Using their templates, designs, and fonts, you can make something awesome for your blog.

I also have great luck on Upwork.com with finding logo artists. My logo for wendyvandepoll.com cost me $20, and people always comment how perfect it is for my brand.

My logos for Center for Pet Loss Grief and Center for Animal Communication cost me more. But when I ordered them, I didn't know about Upwork.

Proudly display your logo on your blog where visitors can see it. You can feature it next to your title and on your home page. The bottom of your page, known as the footer, or the end of your posts are also great places. Find somewhere it stands out.

A visual double entendre is a great place to start. This is where two images come together to make one statement. For instance, a hair brush and a dog imposed over each other could be great for a grooming business, while a snake wrapped around the title of a blog could be great for a snake shop.

Also, use negative space. That's blank space in your logo. It makes the viewer focus upon your actual logo content more.

Symmetry is often vital. A symmetrical image is visually pleasing to people. When you look at it, it should have a nice shape, and its different components should line up or fit together nicely. Custom type that follows the same rules of symmetry is a great way to sum up your blog name in a nice little logo that stands out.

Colors are even more vital. Colors represent messages to people. With a pet blog, figure out the colors that best represent your blog's purpose. If you are writing about animal abuse, red for anger and passion might be appropriate, or gray for sadness and seriousness. Pastel or cartoon designs with bright colors would suit lighter topics.

If you are not a master artist, never fear. You can stick with something simple. Think of the Nike swish: a simple swish design has become one of the most famous logos in history. A simple shape or cartoon is sufficient.

You can also hire a logo designer online or locally and have a professional artist create something more beautiful and complex, if you so desire.

Don't just do what everyone else is doing. You want something recognizable. When people see it, they think of you. Think of some popular logos, like the Starbucks mermaid or the Evernote elephant head. Both are clear, and both are recognizable. Your logo should be like that.

Adding motion or activity is also great. More active logos inspire action in viewers. A cartoon dog who is clearly running is an example. Maybe show a cat meowing, indicated by noise lines or a cartoon speaking bubble over its head.

Fill a few notebooks with sketches. Look at other pet bloggers' logos to ensure you are not copying anyone. Once you find something unique and symmetrical, you can design it.

STICK TO YOUR NICHE

Since you have already established your niche, you want to generally stay within it. You will throw readers off if they follow you for excellent dog advice and you start writing about cats. You can even lose readers if they feel that your information is too off-topic and they are no longer getting what they signed up for.

When you get an idea for a blog post, think about whether or not it relates to your niche and furthers your blog's purpose. You can do things a bit differently now and then, but you can generally find the most success by delivering on what you originally promised readers you would.

If you decide to shake things up, be sure to say in the intro to your post, "I'm doing something a bit different today!"

Incongruent ideas don't have to be rejected. Maybe you should create another blog for them. Just don't jumble tons of unrelated ideas in the same blog, or you will confuse and lose your readers.

START WRITING

Don't know what to write about? Get a blank page. Then start writing words that come to mind. Eventually, an idea will take shape. This works almost every time for me.

I like to collect ideas in a notebook or record them on my phone. When I'm out of things to write about, I revisit my old ideas and expand on them, turning them into blog posts. Never let an idea go to waste. Always document it for later.

When I'm truly dry in the idea well, which is rare, I like to go do something or talk to someone for inspiration. New experiences give you unique stories. Maybe volunteer at the shelter, watch a pet movie, or visit a friend. Look into trends and read about current disagreements on issues that have people talking. These things can give you inspiring topics to research.

FIND TRENDING TOPICS

If something is trending, that means everyone is looking it up. It would be wise to hop on the bandwagon. However, don't base your blog solely on a trend, since trends fade away. A few posts dedicated to a trend should be good enough to draw in new readers.

You can tell something is trending when you see it time and again on other blogs and in social media. Your social media groups will reference it. Your other pet friends will mention it. You can also look at hashtags (Glossary) on Facebook and Twitter to see if any current trending ones relate to your niche.

A still current yet long-term trend is feeding a raw diet to our dogs and cats. Maybe feature an article on this or offer some reviews of popular books on the topic by the experts.

Another big trend involves huskies, after Game of Thrones. Appeal to the Game of Thrones pet lovers and new or aspiring husky owners by writing about how many people don't know how to properly care for huskies and how the number of unwanted huskies going to shelters is rapidly rising. Feature an article on how to care for huskies the right way.

The trend should obviously fit into your particular niche in the pet industry, of course. Writing about huskies in a fish blog is obviously not appropriate. Find trends in your own niche and you will have a wealth of things to write about.

Maybe every month, look into new trends and dedicate at least one post to it. That way, you stay current with the times and continue to produce content that readers find relevant. Be flexible and open to the changing times, and then your blog will weather the test of time!

PERSONAL STORIES

My favorite thing to do while blogging is sharing my own pet stories. As a pet lover, your ticket to many readers is relating to them on the nuances and joys of pet ownership. Sharing your stories will most definitely appeal to people and incur readers!

Photos or videos accompanying these posts are even more winning. A photo of your naughty dog after she ate the trash, followed by an amusing anecdote about the incident and how you subsequently remedied her trash-eating behavior, is great.

A little story about your lizard's finicky treatment of crickets, followed by a photo of her in her cage with live crickets hopping around before your review of a certain lizard feeding method or food product, is another great example.

Accompany a post with a story about how the topic is relevant to you. Share your experiences with said topic. Give readers something person to relate to. Then they feel more inclined to read on because they think, "This is like something that happened to me!" Even just bringing a smile to someone's face will make readers read on.

I like to begin a post with some sort of relatable story. As I relate the story, readers feel hooked to read on because they want to know the ending. The ending can be the overall point you want to make.

You can show how you made a mistake with your pet and what you learned, or what you did that worked in your favor. You can share research you performed to figure out how to surmount some new challenge with a pet. You can recommend products that address the main problem in your story.

Your personal story should have some basic point. Otherwise, readers will wonder, "Why did I just waste so much time reading this for nothing?" Have an introduction, a problem, and a remedy. Use that to lead into the topic you are writing about in your post.

Some blogs are built entirely on sharing amusing stories. You can build a readership just by sharing funny pictures, videos, memes, and stories about your pets or your experiences with pets.

If you do this, however, you must dedicate the blog to that. Throwing in random articles about other topics will throw off readers who feel committed to reading about your pet and only your pet.

These blogs thrive because people love animals. As they follow your blog, they feel as if they are part of your pet's life. They become emotionally invested. That is how you keep readers coming back, by creating emotional investment.

Regular updates and sharing cute stories will make them keep reading. When your pet passes away, they will grieve with you. You can create a massive support community based on your pet, with people sharing their own stories and expressing lots of love for your pet.

One thing I really love to do is illustrate how I made a mistake and how I learned from it. Readers love this because you show your vulnerability—you are not some perfect, untouchable pet guru, but rather a real person who is capable of making mistakes and bouncing back.

People will find that far more relatable, and they will derive comfort from the fact that you made the same mistake they have made. Show people that they can recover and learn from mistakes by describing how you did.

RHETORICAL APPEAL

Any writer can benefit from a crash course on ethos, pathos, and logos. These three elements of rhetoric are taught in basic English classes, then quickly forgotten. However, they are key to creating written content and pictures that people become invested in. To keep readers coming back, you should employ these elements in your posts. That is how you become *riveting*!

Ethos

Ethos involves appealing to the ethics of readers. As a pet writer, your readers are going to care most about the ethical implications certain people or practices have regarding animals.

Bringing attention to the harm certain training or feeding trends has on animals can persuade readers to find something better. Calling out some organization for animal testing or cruelty is another way to convince readers to boycott that company.

Don't just point out the dismal unethical treatment of roosters in cock fighting rings, for example. Point out a solution. Highlight an organization or product that helps.

Help people see how they can right an ethical wrongdoing. Readers will become hooked, as they want to read how to solve an ethical problem they care about.

For instance, if you are writing about how hitting your puppy during house training is wrong, point out why it hurts a puppy's psychology and his bond with his owner, and then offer a different way to train using positive reinforcement.

Pathos

Pathos is the emotional side of your writing. You want to make readers feel what you are writing about. If you are raising awareness about how important it is to neuter and spay, you should invoke emotions in pet owners. Prove to them that pets suffer from overpopulation.

A picture of an overcrowded local shelter, a moving paragraph about the lack of funding and suffering animals endure in shelters, and a bit about how pets are euthanized due to overpopulation will make pet owners feel horrible for other animals. They will then be more inclined to neuter or spay. Pathos is how you can make a difference.

Pathos doesn't have to be all negative. You can make people feel warm and fuzzy inside, which in turn drives them to keep reading to brighten their days. You can make people feel like good pet owners. That praise can make them want to return to your blog for more. Offer something emotional and you will get readers.

Logos

Logos is logic. The logical side of anything involves the facts, the research, the statistics. Some people find logic more appealing than emotions. But even people who are more invested in your blog emotionally can benefit from some solid facts.

Providing advice, statistics, facts, and research results can educate readers and show them what to do. Direct them toward a product or cause that you may be supporting by using pathos or ethos or both, suggesting a solution, and then showing the evidence supporting a solution.

For instance, if you are pushing for people to donate to the Humane

Society, you should combine these three elements. Show how pets suffer from abuse to appeal to both pathos and ethos. Then make people feel good by showing them what the Humane Society does. Then break it down into math, or logos, by showing how much money the Society needs to raise for something and where that money goes.

START WRITING

Before you even begin to write your post, you must brainstorm what it will be about. Ideally, you have a topic picked out. But now you must ask yourself, "What do I want my readers to know after reading my post?"

A blog can flop horribly if the writer doesn't think of this. People don't want to waste their time reading meandering posts that never teach anything or make any solid points.

They also get frustrated if the blog makes a point, jumps to a wildly different point, circles back to the first point, comes out of left field with some odd bit of information, and goes on and on, jumping around between topics.

To make your blog post worth reading, decide on at least four takeaways the reader should gain from your blog (more is better!). These are four things you want your readers to learn or do. Write them down. If one takeaway is unrelated to the overall topic of the post, cut it. Your post needs to stay on topic and not shift to other things, or you could lose the reader.

For example, if you are discussing natural flea treatments for a kitty, you want to come up with the four basic takeaways relating only to feline flea treatments: natural products don't harm your pets as much as chemicals; flea treatments are necessary only when your cat has a flea infestation; which products are best to use; how effective these products are and any tips you may have for using them.

After you have outlined your takeaways, you can add more information with your research, knowledge, and tips in more detail. This way, you know when and where to insert certain information in a logical way.

Also, consider how each subtopic ties into the next. That way, you can create a nice flow for your post. It would be most logical to start by talking about what flea dips are and how they contain dangerous chemicals, which you can then segue into an introduction to natural products.

Since you are still trying to convince readers to use a natural product over a dangerous chemical, you should probably place the takeaway about effectiveness here. Then go into how often you should dip and which products to use. Include tips with each product you feature.

Do you see how flow can be achieved by logically linking the different main points of your post? Think of how one topic relates to another to create flow.

Also think where in the post a topic may be most effective. Least important points should go toward the end, while more important ones (or ones "selling" an idea to the readers) should go toward the top.

Finally, decide on headings for each takeaway. Break the takeaway into different paragraphs, with a clear heading that uses a keyword and describes the point of the paragraph.

Separating paragraphs with headings is a great way to sneak in some SEO and give your post a clean appearance.

OVERALL BLOG POST LAYOUT

Before you start writing, you can generate an outline that organizes your points into a neat structure that readers can easily follow. You can rearrange the outline as needed until the post has a logical flow.

It's always better to have one topic lead into the next, such as a paragraph about training your puppy to come to his name followed by one about how to accomplish that. If you use a logical sequence, where one topic builds upon the previous one, you create a post that is easier to read.

You don't have to follow an outline format to the letter. But having a formula for how you usually lay out your posts can be extremely helpful, especially on those days when you're crunched for time but you have to post something.

It prevents you from missing key elements of your post or skipping over important parts. You also don't have to think as hard when you post.

HERE'S WHAT THE TYPICAL OUTLINE SHOULD LOOK LIKE:

- **Introduction**

Here is where you state what your post is going to be about. You want to introduce the topic to readers in a way that hooks them to read more.

Use some keywords and some sort of lead-in. I love to use a question like, "What do you do when your new puppy pees in the house?"

The introduction should also make some sort of promise. "In this post, I'm going to show you how to house train your new puppy effectively and humanely." Share what you have to offer and why readers will benefit if they read on.

Always focus on what readers have to gain from reading your post! It is shameless self-advertising that puts you out there.

Finally, use a call to action. This may be something like "Read on to find out more!" or "Let's end this abuse now!" The call to action makes readers want to take action by reading more, in order to make some sort of change or solve a problem.

Think of introductions like this: A reader is skimming the intro, wondering if he or she should dedicate time to finishing the post. You must make the reader want to finish it.

Therefore, your intro must "sell" the rest of the post. A clear statement of the subject, a promise for how this post will help readers, and a call to action are how you do this.

- **First Topic**

Separate your first paragraph from your introduction using a heading. Then launch into your first, and most important, subtopic. Offer as many details and facts as you can.

Images and videos are often attention-grabbers. Plus, people prefer shorter paragraphs. Don't have long paragraphs with more than four sentences. Once you start a new train of thought, definitely start a new paragraph.

- **Second Topic**

Separate your second subtopic from the first with another heading. Then repeat. Keep doing this for each new subtopic. Make your main points and focus on providing one of the takeaways you outlined with each subtopic.

- **Conclusion**

In my writing experience, most people have the most trouble with conclusions. But conclusions are actually very easy to write! All you have to do is sum up everything you just said in a neat little sentence or two.

Then invite readers to chime in or encourage them to tell you about their results with the last sentence. Three to four sentences are sufficient.

You must include a conclusion with each post. It reminds readers of what you just said, and it leaves them with a sense of completion. Some people only read conclusions as a way to rapidly get information about the whole post.

USE CONSTRUCTIVE FEEDBACK

As you gain a following, you might get lots of requests. "I want to know more about…" or "Could you post more about…?" These comments are the most valuable tools you have as a blogger.

They can hurt, sure. You want people to just accept what you have to say, and you don't like being told that they want something else.

But as a blogger, the only way to grow your business is by giving your followers answers to what they are asking. So, if your readers are clamoring for something, or voicing complaints, you can use that feedback to power new content.

The great thing about blogs is that they are malleable to change with the times. The blog that endures the test of time is the one that is flexible to change. You would be wise to make adjustments where they are needed.

If something doesn't fly with readers, you can remove it. If readers want more of something, give it to them. Make the changes that people want to see.

Now, if you have one bizarre suggestion from one person, and no one else says the same thing, then you can safely disregard it. Don't do things that disagree with you emotionally or morally, or that seem outlandish or ill-fitting for your blog. Don't do things that seem totally unnecessary or incongruent with your niche, either. You don't have to cater to each and every single reader of your blog. Stay true to yourself.

In the blogging world, you can encounter some weird things. Some people are trolls, only out to hurt others with mean-spirited comments. Other people have strange ideas that they insist you use.

Yet others don't seem to actually read your content before they post totally irrelevant comments. Be sure to take everything you read on your blog's comments with a little caution.

But popular opinion, or the majority vote, can really suggest a change is in order. If most readers are somehow dissatisfied with something you have posted, then you should take that into consideration. Use it as a chance to help yourself elevate your blog.

For example, maybe you post a recipe for doggie biscuits. A ton of users complain that they can't find a specific ingredient in their local grocery stores, or they complain that the instructions didn't work. You may need to revise the recipe to fit the needs of the majority. Add a more common ingredient or post where people can order the rare ingredient online. Clarify instructions or find where you went wrong.

You may have people asking lots of questions that your blog post should have answered. If lots of people don't seem to be getting what you say, it may be time to clarify a few points with more specific language, or even bolding a part so that readers pay attention to it.

People may complain that your post did not provide enough information. It can't hurt making another post addressing the information that people want. Prove to your readers that you listen and you care by addressing their concerns.

PROOFREAD WITH SOFTWARE

I am an advocate for intuitive writing. This is where you write without pausing to fix grammar or criticize yourself. Doing this lets you get your ideas out. You don't ever stop yourself to fix a spelling error, or else you throttle the flow of ideas.

The problem with this is that your writing may come out jumbled, phrased oddly, and full of errors. That's okay, though. That's where editing comes in.

Before you post something, you must edit it. Poor writing is frustrating to read. You can lose followers if your posts are not high quality. Therefore, you must polish your posts after you write them to ensure that they read nicely, with no distracting errors.

It can be easy to overlook simple mistakes if you are the author of a post. You know what you meant to say in your mind, so you skip over flaws in your writing, missing words, or even misspellings. That is where an editing software comes in handy.

I use ProWritingAid (Resources). It is a plug-in that you can add to your browser, Google documents, and Microsoft Office. It also has a desktop application where you can edit documents from your computer.

ProWritingAid checks for spelling and grammar errors in your writing and offers suggestions for improvement. You even get notifications about run-on sentences and improper verb tenses!

My advice is to create your blog posts in a word processor. Then run it through ProWritingAid. The result will be a polished post that you can then copy and paste into your post editor on WordPress.

PUBLISH YOUR CONTENT

This is your last step to creating great content: publishing it!

The sense of bravery and accomplishment you feel when you make your first post public is exhilarating. You just became a part of the Internet. Thousands, even millions, of people can now see what you have written.

You just put yourself out there and started growing your own Internet community. You are reaching out to others and making yourself known. Plus, you are one step closer to gaining followers and monetizing your blog!

WRAP-UP

In this chapter, you learned about creating a riveting blog post. You must find inspiration and begin organizing your thoughts. Put them into a logical outline. Then let the words flow.

Afterward, you can use a proofreading software to correct your piece. You can also make sure it logically fits in with your post's theme and uses ethos, pathos, and logos.

Once you have written your piece, publish it. Then use the feedback you get to improve your blog. You should stay true to yourself, but also hear what your readers have to say. Your readers are the ones who promote your blog and make you money, so give them what they really want!

Use the action steps at the end of this chapter as a checklist for getting your article written and ready for your followers.

In Chapter 6, you will learn how to pair social media with your blog to increase your readership and gain more followers.

Social media offers you free and paid advertising options that are extremely effective. Read on to learn how to create your very own brand on social media!

ACTION STEPS

> Listed are the steps I covered in this chapter. Use the action steps as a checklist as you proceed with creating your blog. Refer back in this chapter to gain more detail when you are ready for the tasks outlined below.

Step 1: Create a Logo

Step 2: Gather Inspiration

Step 3: Brainstorm and Create an Outline

Step 4: Write Intuitively

Step 5: See if it Fits Your Niche

Step 6: Proofread it

Step 7: Listen to Critics and Fans Alike

Step 8: Publish!

III

GROWING YOUR BLOG FOR SUCCESS

6

GETTING SOCIAL WITH SOCIAL MEDIA

Friendship is born at that moment when one person says to another, What! You, too? I thought I was the only one. — C.S. Lewis

Think about the brands that you know. What makes you buy them again and again? Probably the quality, the customer service, the company's values, and even the marketing. Prices and availability probably also factor into your brand loyalty.

When it comes to your blog, you are a brand yourself. You offer people information. If you do so in a way that people find trustworthy and appealing, more people will trust your brand and follow you for years!

They will follow you because of the confidence you developed with them, and they will sign up for the products or courses you offer.

Now why do you ditch brands? The main reason is probably a decline in quality, availability, or even company values and customer care. The same goes for your brand. If your blog dips in quality or anything else that you have promised your readers, you will start to lose people.

It is important to roll with the times. But don't change so much that old fans lose interest. Always keep an element of what you started with, whatever makes your blog unique.

To cement your brand and raise awareness about it, you should use social media to connect with potential readers. Social media allows you to build an online personality and presence that readers can identify with.

It helps promote you as an online influencer, or person that people want to follow. Your blog shows your voice; your social media shows your presence. Often, no one will ever discover your blog unless you promote it with social media.

THE IMPORTANCE OF SOCIAL MEDIA TRAFFIC

Why all this fuss about social media, you wonder? Well, the more people who visit your blog, the higher your blog ranks in searches.

That means you reach more people, make more of a difference, and start getting enough attention to monetize your blog, which is covered more extensively in Chapter 8. As you reach people, your readership and your email list will grow.

Social media is a great way to reach more people and start to drive traffic to your blog. It puts your brand in front of people.

Many of your readers will come from social media. As they see you on social media, they feel inclined to click on your posts, which takes them to your blog. Your following on various social platforms directly translates to people visiting your blog.

Social media followers are in addition to your email list when you consider the number of people following you. Just because someone isn't on your list doesn't mean that they don't still keep an eye on you through social media.

As people see your promotions and new posts, they access your content, just as someone who receives your emails does. You get attention and reach many people this way. The goal, however, is to get the folks on social media to sign up for your newsletter.

A social media presence also puts you in the center of activity relating to your niche. You get to connect with people who love pets as much as you do. You can take part in fun social media groups, where you can garner attention for your blog with authoritative posts.

In addition, you get to meet other bloggers, some of whom can become lifelong colleagues. When new trends or content enter the Internet world, you can be among the first to learn about them and feature them in your blog. Comments on social media can tune you into trends, as well as what your readers think of your posts.

CREATING SOCIAL MEDIA PAGES

To thrive in the blogosphere, you must create pages on the main social media giants right now. These are Twitter, Instagram, Tumblr, LinkedIn, and Facebook. Less than a decade ago, Myspace was big, but now it is obsolete.

Maybe one day, Twitter and Facebook will become obsolete as users drift to another social media trend, so stay on top of this. Whatever social media becomes hot in your niche, make sure you have a presence on it!

If you don't already have accounts on these social media companies, create ones now. You can build a business page from your personal account on Facebook. Otherwise, you can create new accounts for your blog.

You have two options here. You could create an account under your name or under your blog name. It is best to create one dedicated solely to your business, unless your personal name and your business name are clearly linked.

For instance, my blog's URL is wendyvandepoll.com, and my name is Wendy Van de Poll. It is obvious that I am the same person. However, with my blog centerforpetlossgrief.com, it wouldn't make sense to link people to social media pages bearing my personal name.

Obviously, you don't want to link people to your personal social media account, the one you share with friends and family. You want to create a business page dedicated entirely to your business.

The reason for this is twofold: For one thing, you will be connecting with lots of strangers, so you don't want people you don't know personally having access to pictures of your house and your grandkids for security reasons!

Additionally, your followers want to see things relating to your blog, not your personal life. This doesn't mean that you can never put personal posts on your business page. Your followers want to know who the person is behind all your great blogs. Remember to keep it professional and have your "personal" post relate to your brand.

BUILDING YOUR BRAND ON SOCIAL MEDIA

Your social media accounts should bear the same logo and colors and even pictures as your blog. That way, users know that they are in the right place. Consistency in your brand is key. You must keep the same appearance across all interfaces.

On your page, you will have to create your profile. Fill it out with details about your blog and its theme, followed by a paragraph about you.

Tell readers what to expect and why they should trust you as an authority in a particular niche. Use a photo of you as your picture, and create a cover photo using your main blog photo. Write your bio in the same voice that you use in your blog across all social media to build further consistency within your brand.

There will also be a place to enter your URL. You want to first enter your blog's URL. That way, people can find you easily. You can also connect the URLs to other social media accounts.

In addition to decorating your page just like your blog, you should also post about your blog. These posts will generate interest and drive traffic to your blog.

For every post, you should feature the featured WordPress picture, a summary of what your post is about, and an easy link that people can click on to reach your blog.

Don't give away your content for free! Offer a teaser. Say something like, "Make your own dog treats!" Then feature a few lines of the recipe and a link to your blog post. People have to click on it to see more. If you feature the whole recipe, then people won't bother going to your blog post.

Why visit your blog when you feature all of it on social media? Drive traffic to your blog with little teasers that make people want to visit your blog for more.

You can also garner more attention by posting content and links relevant to your brand. Say you run a blog dedicated to ending safari hunting and trophy hunting. Sharing articles about this subject on your social media page can help build awareness about your cause and make more people visit your profile.

As people come to appreciate the content you post, they will be more likely to check out your blog.

Be sure to interact with people, as well. Like and comment on their posts. Post things asking people about their opinions or post surveys and polls to gain information about popular opinions.

Facebook has automated polls, which you can create within a post. The more you interact with people, the more connections you make. These connections draw people to look into your blog.

Join groups on social media. LinkedIn and Facebook are known for groups. When you join groups, become active in them. This establishes you as an authority and makes people aware of who you are.

When you join groups and comment people begin to recognize your page name and feel more familiar with it when they check out your blog. This is just another way to cement your brand on social media.

Facebook and Instagram feature ads. For a small fee, you can appear as an ad on the feeds of social media users. If someone looks up a lot of dog-related information and you run a blog about dogs, Facebook will put you in front of someone's eyes. Running ads is a great way to get people to know about your blog.

Finally, host events. You may host a watch party for a live video where you demonstrate how to groom a cat without getting scratched, for instance. Advertise that watch party on your blog and all of your social media accounts with a link and a time.

You may also host a product review party or a special on some product you sell. You may advertise a free consultation session. Creating public events, such as "Dog Park Day," can help you connect with local people.

I'm going to include some instructions for each social media brand that is big right now. If you are using social media interfaces that I don't cover here, be sure to get comfortable with them and follow similar tips when creating a blog page.

The basic premise is the same: Establish who you are and what your blog is about consistently across all social media to create a recognizable brand that resonates with people.

FACEBOOK

From your personal Facebook account, you can create a business page for your blog. Be sure to add a photo of you as a profile picture and use your blog's name as the page name.

Feature a link to your blog in the "Website" blank and fill out the long and short descriptions of your blog. Under "About Me," talk about why you write this blog, your mission, and how you are qualified.

Use Facebook ads to reach more people. Also, join Facebook groups and get active on relevant content. Post things every day. Post every time you make a new blog post.

Start by inviting your friends to like you. Also, like other blogs on related topics. That way, more people see your blog and are likely to "like" you. Once people like you, they will see your content on their feeds. This is a great promotional opportunity.

TWITTER

Tweet often, and tweet well. Every time you make a new post, be sure to tweet about it.

Make your profile all about your blog. Feature your logo and a description and link to your blog. Also link to all of your other social media accounts.

Inside your blog, feature a link to Twitter with your other social media buttons. Your "Contact Me" page is great for this, as well as the footer of your site.

Follow lots of other active Twitter users in your niche. Refer to your blog in your comments, without making it obvious. For instance, you can say, "I actually wrote about this in my blog recently! I can't agree with you more."

Constantly posting links to your blog can get you banned for spam, but sneaking in references to your blog won't do this. Retweet things major influencers post, as well, to get more attention.

Join Twitter chats. Add valuable input on these chats and you'll make friends and even be invited as a guest on a chat.

Be sure to follow lots of people. That way, people follow you. Expand beyond your circle by following strangers who show an interest in pets.

INSTAGRAM

Instagram is dedicated to photos. To keep your Instagram account going, be sure to post lots of pet pictures with a link to your newest blog posts in the caption. Instagram is a fun platform and very pet friendly.

Also, be sure to use some copywriting techniques by writing short and concise sentences. "Today I'll show you how to make dog cookies!" with a picture of you and your dog in the kitchen is a great example.

Show people what your post is about and how they will benefit from reading it. Make your copy short and sweet and to the point.

In your Instagram profile, feature your logo as the profile picture. Use a handle that is your name or your blog name condensed, like your URL. Finally, be sure to put your blog's URL and write about the things your blog offers under "About Me." Write a bit about who you are and why you are qualified to be running this blog here, as well.

Feature a "Follow Me on Instagram!" button on your blog. This helps people easily connect with you by one click.

And don't forget about hashtags—Instagram allows thirty hashtags (see Glossary).

LINKEDIN

LinkedIn is a social networking site for professionals. To promote your business, definitely create a LinkedIn profile. On the profile, talk about your expertise and feature a link to your blog.

As you add new followers, be sure to send an email greeting each new member by name and then invite them to look at your blog. Talk a bit about what your blog features and how they will benefit from following you.

It is helpful to create a basic email template. Copy and paste that to each new email you send out. Customize the name and you're good to go!

Post every day or every other day. Talk about your newest blog post or some issue that you will be discussing soon. That way, LinkedIn users can follow your content on LinkedIn and tune into your blog when you post something relevant to them.

Add a LinkedIn button to your blog. The bottom of your blog is an ideal place, as well as on your "Contact Me" page. Include the URL to your LinkedIn profile.

SET A SCHEDULE

To remain relevant on social media, you must post often. The easiest way to stay on top of posts is to automate them. But you also want to post personal things directly to add a more relatable human element to your social media brand.

How can you remember to spend all this time posting on social media if you also have to run your blog, answer emails, *and* all the other numerous tasks and events in your busy schedule? I've certainly been there.

Sometimes, you just don't feel that you have the time. However, since social media is so important to building your online brand and web presence, it is worthy of you making time for it.

Set a schedule. Follow it closely. Dedicate maybe an hour a day to posting, chatting, and commenting on your different social media accounts. Consider it all part of a day's work!

AUTOMATE SOCIAL MEDIA POSTS

When you create a new post on WordPress, you can then go and manually post a link to your blog with a teaser on all of your social media accounts. Or, you can save tons of time by automating the social media posting! Never forget to post again, as a handy software can handle all of that for you.

Here's how to automate social media posts from within your blog: Get

Agora Pulse. Then set a schedule and link up to six social media accounts across the web. Specify what you want the posts to say.

You can even assign different users if you're working with a team. Agora Pulse does the rest! There is also the option to analyze the success of your posts and get free tips on how to improve your posts.

Agora Pulse is not the only social media posting software out there. You can also try Hootsuite, Buffer, or Crowdfire. They all work in roughly the same way. Try them out and see which ones are easiest for you.

Be sure to add some variety to your automated posts so that your posts seem more personal and your followers don't get bored of the same content over and over. Each post should be unique.

GET FOLLOWERS ON SOCIAL MEDIA

Let's get a little more in depth about how to attract followers on social media.

No one is going to follow you if they don't know you exist. A lack of followers hardly means that your social media brand is lackluster. It just means that you need to put yourself out there a little more and get yourself in front of people.

First, remember the demographic you identified in Chapter 2? That demographic applies to your social media brand, as well. Write to the demographic your niche appeals to with your social posts.

Next, be sure to post meaningful content. No one bothers to read novels on social media. Short, visual posts gain way more attention. A featured photo of a cute pet and a snappy title that summarizes your blog post is great.

But also consider graphs, infographics, or factual videos that offer teasers about your post's content. Sometimes, you can also just post a link to your blog featuring your logo and a teaser like, "Want to learn how to train your dog? Visit my blog!"

Keywords summarized as hashtags will make you appear in social media searches. When someone clicks on a hashtag, they will see your post on the results. Be sure to find relevant hashtags and add them to the end of your posts.

Occasionally, offer a poll. Or offer a contest. "First hundred visitors who sign up for my newsletter get a free gift!" is a good example. This way, you engage readers and give them a reason to visit your blog.

Also, use your keywords generously in your posts. Social media posts on public profiles will show up on search engine searches. Your posts should be retrieved with a keyword. More people will find you if you optimize your posts.

WRAP-UP

Social media is a critical part of getting a readership for your blog. You must feature your blog on all social media. Make it easy for people to follow your accounts from your blog, too.

Engage your audience with meaningful posts. Interact with them through games, contests, polls, and other such posts. Be sure to update them when you post something new to the blog. Posting on a schedule keeps your followers engaged and your social media accounts populated.

Social media lets you find lots of people who may be interested in your blog. You can use it to create your brand, your web presence, and your readership.

Review the action steps for this chapter to keep you on track for your planning.

Now, read on to learn how to retain readers who visit your blog.

Getting people to come back to your blog is the foundation for blogging success!

ACTION STEPS

> *Listed are the steps I covered in this chapter. Use the action steps as a checklist as you proceed with creating your blog. Refer back in this chapter to gain more detail when you are ready for the tasks outlined below.*

Step 1: Start social media accounts for your business. Twitter, Facebook, LinkedIn, and Instagram are good places to start.

Step 2: Drive traffic with your social media. Add friends, appeal to followers, and post updates.

Step 3: Set a schedule. You must post in a timely manner to engage with your followers.

Step 4: Get more followers. Offer polls, free gifts, and great content. Use keywords and hashtags to show up higher in searchers. Post in relevant groups to draw attention to your site. Every new follower is a potential lead!

7

GET THEM TO COME BACK!

Every contact we have with a customer influences whether or not they'll come back. We have to be great every time or we'll lose them. — Kevin Stirtz

Recurring readers is a sign that your blog is doing well. If people keep coming back for more, then they are clearly invested in your brand and loyal to you. But how do you get people to come back?

I'm sure you have visited plenty of blogs in your time. You may have liked what you read. However, it was not easy to follow the blog, so you left to visit other sites and you forgot about it.

Then maybe you attempted to look it up again, but it had already become lost in cyberspace, buried by newer posts. If only you could remember its name...

I'm sure you have also visited blogs that you quickly backed out of in search of something better. Maybe the blog was too brief to be informative, or maybe it was poorly written, or maybe its tone just didn't appeal to you.

The key here is to avoid the two scenarios above. To get people to come back, you want to offer a convenient way to sign up and social media links so that people can follow you.

It is important to offer some sort of incentive, such as a discount code or free report, can get more people to give their emails to your ever-growing email list.

You also want to offer content and a layout that makes people stick around to read more. Deliver consistently good, informative, and well-written content, and you get consistently loyal readers.

COLLECT EMAILS

When people visit your blog, you want to have a highly visible place for them to subscribe to your newsletter by giving their email. This is a surefire way to keep putting your content in front of people. By making it easy for people to subscribe to your list, you enable people to actually sign up.

Once someone subscribes to you, this person becomes a lead. Generating leads involves making it easy and convenient for people to subscribe. If you can continue to put meaningful content before them, these leads then become customers.

Also, make it easy for people to follow you on social media. That makes it even more possible to place content in front of them that they will want to read. I recommend placing social media links in handy buttons at the bottom or top of every page on your site.

SharedCounts is a convenient plug-in that places social media buttons of any style you choose wherever you want on your site. Or if you are using Avada (Chapter 4), this is already built in for you.

How do you collect emails? That part is easy! I use ConvertKit (Resources), which is a great way to move visitors into leads. MailChimp is also a great option, with some limitations. MailChimp is free for under two thousand subscribers, but becomes expensive with over two thousand.

That's why I recommend ConvertKit. I also have found that ConvertKit is more robust for a monthly fee. Again, I won't go into fees here since they may change with time, but I find them to be reasonable for the amount of return I get from them!

ConvertKit is actually a WordPress plug-in. Install it from your plug-ins on your dashboard. Once it downloads, hit "Activate."

Now create an account and log in to it to access your API key. Within your account, you will find a button that says, "Show Secret." Click on it and you will retrieve your API key, which you can then copy and paste into the API key blank in your WordPress.

In your settings, you can choose a form and where it appears. You can post one with every blog post, as well as on every page of your blog. You can customize forms to fit different types of posts or different pages, as well.

If you choose to use MailChimp instead, you can also install the plug-in.

With these handy forms, you can get visitors to give you their emails. Then you can send them updates when you post a new thing to your blog, as well as advertisements for different things you may offer, such as coupon codes to an affiliate company or a new course. More on that in the next chapter!

GENERATE DISCUSSIONS

When you are posting, be sure to engage your readers. Interacting with readers helps you establish great business connections, plus it makes your readers feel as if they are actually getting something back from your blog.

Having a great business relationship with your readers inspires a sense of trust, which in turn inspires loyalty!

When you make a post, think of a way to engage your readers. You might host a contest on social media or on your blog. Get people to post pictures with their pets, for instance, and have them vote on pictures to find a winner.

This could even be a weekly thing! The winner could be featured on your home page and receive some sort of gift, such as a coupon code or a free product.

You might ask readers a question and encourage them to answer in the comments. Generate healthy discussions by asking for opinions.

You might tell readers that you will share top comments in your next post. Then, people will comment more meaningful things in order to be featured in your next post.

You can even have a live chat, where you answer questions and comments. You can do this on social media, but be sure to announce it from your blog and let readers know when and where the chat will be online.

Finally, you can offer free (or paid) consultations. If people have pet questions, tell them to please email you. You can email back and forth or set up video conferences where you answer their burning pet questions.

These are just a few ideas. The way you interact with people will depend on your blog and your demographic. Find a way that works for you and makes your blog both interactive and fun.

STAY ON TOP OF COMMENTS

The comments on your articles are a way for you to gain valuable feedback and connect with your readers in a more personal way.

The Internet world can be lonely with no personal communication or it can be warm and full of potential relationships. Replying to comments and engaging with readers personally will make your blog interactive and fun.

Readers will appreciate hearing from you. If you reply to a comment or even email a person back about a comment, you make a personal connection that validates that person's presence on your blog.

Be sure to change your settings to "Approve Comments" so that you can disapprove spam or abusive comments. You don't want your blog becoming cluttered with irrelevant or offensive comments, as that can deter other readers. Always censor comments before you approve them!

To do this, go to your WordPress settings. Click on "Discussion" and then "Before a comment appears." Check the box next to "Comment must be manually approved." Then hit "Save Changes" at the bottom of the page and test it out for yourself by posting a comment. You should get an email asking if you want to approve the comment. Now you have the power to approve or disapprove all comments!

This can get a bit overwhelming when you are running a high-volume blog. If you don't want to spend most of your day sifting through comments, repeat the steps above and be sure to change the settings from "Comment must be manually approved" to "Comment author must have previously approved comment." That automates comment approval from people you know and trust on your blog.

When people post a comment, they will have to enter their email. That makes it easy to add them to your list. You can also send them a Captcha (Glossary) to ensure that they are real people, not bots posting spam on numerous pages.

SET ASIDE TIME FOR EMAILS

As you get personal emails, you must reply to them. You can automate a reply that lets a person know that you have received the email and will respond soon. That reply can make people feel more patient, since they have received something from you.

Set aside some time each day to answer emails. Giving your readers your attention inspires yet more loyalty. You can help people by chatting with them, answering their questions, and getting involved.

Have a goal for the number of emails you answer each day. It can be time-consuming if you get a lot of emails, so start from the oldest and work your way up. Be sure to read each email completely in order to come up with a relevant reply.

Send thoughtful replies with good content, written in the voice you use for your blog. Address each email personally to each person, so that you don't appear cold and impersonal.

Sign them warmly with your blogging name or personal name, depending which one you are using online, and something like "Warmly" or "Wishing the best." You can also ask for updates to inspire a sense of caring in your correspondence.

Stamp your emails with a cute pet-related .gif or your logo. That way, your brand sticks with people and your emails adhere to your blog's voice.

HOW TO AUTOMATE EMAILS

ConvertKit allows you to send beautiful emails on a schedule to keep up with your readers. From within ConvertKit, you can create newsletter forms that you simply fill out. You also can set up automatic emails, such as a welcome email that goes out to new subscribers.

First, set a schedule. Readers love consistency, so sending out emails on a consistent schedule inspires more loyalty. People know when to expect to hear from you. Faithfully stick to this schedule, unless you have a surprise that you must update your readers on.

Second, follow the workflow in your ConvertKit account. This shows you what emails are due. You can click on an item and edit it in the same window. This allows you to edit emails as needed before sending them out.

Third, let ConvertKit handle the rest. You will even see a chart showing how well your emails are doing and how many subscribers are completing steps in the emails.

You can also edit outcomes, events, and actions to automate what your readers are supposed to do. The event could be something like a live video on Facebook that you want your readers to join. An action could be as simple as clicking on a new post or joining an online course you are offering.

HAVE A SURVEY WHEN PEOPLE UNSUBSCRIBE

In a perfect world, no one ever hits "Unsubscribe Here" on your emails. But it can and will happen. The best thing you can do is find out why people do this. That can help you improve your emails and avoid more people from unsubscribing.

A simple automatic email response with a survey is easy to set up within ConvertKit. From there, you can gather data on why people are unsubscribing.

Sometimes, people just don't find your content relevant. If that keeps happening, you may want to reevaluate what you are posting to be more relevant to readers.

Other times, people feel that you send too many emails. Maybe you should scale back. I found that once a week to every other week is ideal for my niche. Too many emails start to overload readers and resemble spam.

Maybe you push selling things a little too hard. I like to provide some valuable content in each email and *then* mention something I'm selling, like a consulting session or a course, at the end. I sell myself by offering good content and thus convincing people to pursue what else I offer.

Finally, maybe you're sending out stuff that has little to do with your blog. This would be a mistake. Don't treat your email list like a group of friends that you should forward every interesting article or funny meme to. Assemble content you want to share that relates specifically to your niche into an email that goes out on a regular schedule.

WRAP-UP

Each person who visits your blog is a potential lead, or customer. To retain people, you must make them value your blog and want to come back to it.

The best way to do this is to get people to sign up for emails so that you can notify them when you post new content and send them marketing emails to get them to spend money on your blog!

Also, create a community. This is where you interact with your readers in some fun way. From contests to simply replying to comments, you will get more loyalty as you engage with people personally.

Stay on top of emails. Send them out on a schedule. ConvertKit can automate emails and create forms that get people to sign up for your emails.

If people do unsubscribe, you want to find out why. That way, you can prevent more people from unsubscribing.

Use the action steps at the end of this chapter as a checklist for getting your article written and ready for your followers.

Now that you know how to retain leads and have a loyal following, you can start to make money off of your blog! Do the five action steps and, to turn blogging into an enriching career, read on!

ACTION STEPS

Listed are the steps I covered in this chapter. Use the action steps as a checklist as you proceed with creating your blog. Refer back in this chapter to gain more detail when you are ready for the tasks outlined below.

Step 1: Make it easy to get subscribers! Use ConvertKit forms or an email provider of your choice to get people to sign up and follow you on social media, as well.

Step 2: Automate emails with ConvertKit or an email provider of your choice. Take the time out of emailing as you generate automatic emails and send out updates or newsletters on a set schedule.

Step 3: Engage your readers. Offer ways for them to interact with you.

Step 4: Always stay on top of comments and emails. When people contact you, get back to them! Show that you are there and you are an active part of their lives.

Step 5: Set up a survey when people unsubscribe. Use that data to improve your emails and to retain more leads.

Remember, if you need more information for your action steps, go back to the beginning of this chapter or watch the videos in ConvertKit.

8

MONETIZING YOUR BLOG

I am open to money coming to me from new ways that I've never imagined.
— Anonymous

Monetizing your blog is the process of developing a system to make income from your hard work. Blogs are not get-rich-quick schemes. But with some work and patience, you can start generating excellent income from it!

The most exciting part of blogging is when you start to see a return for all of your efforts. The hours you put in may feel unrewarded at first, but in time, they will start to pay off very well.

The best part is your blog can become a source of passive income that earns money even while you are sleeping. A lot of hard work at the beginning and staying on top of your blog will lead to income that grows with only some emailing and posting on your part in the future.

Your blog is part of a brand. Your brand sells content. Therefore, your customers are the people who visit your blog and use your content. To make money, you must view each person who visits your blog as a customer. Appeal to this customer and you will see money!

Here is what I do to monetize my blogs. My advice to you as you go through this chapter is to have a notebook ready to jot down your ideas on how you want to monetize. You may not implement all your ideas at once, but in the future, you may want to revisit your original ideas.

LEAD MAGNETS

Each person who reads your emails is a potential customer. To get subscribers to spend money at your blog, you want to convert these potential customers, or leads, into real customers.

Lead magnets are simple ways to get people to sign up for your content. Generally, offering someone a free gift of some type is a great lead magnet.

The free gift doesn't need to be something expensive and fancy. I love to offer people special reports on something, such as what dog foods to avoid when I had my natural pet blog. Invite people to take a brief quiz that you design using a plug-in to generate a free report on how they should be feeding their specific breed of dog, for instance.

You can also offer a fifteen-percent-off coupon, or something similar, to new subscribers. This gets lots of people to sign up and redeem their coupons in your store or affiliate links.

You can even send a basic checklist. "Things to get for a new puppy" or "What you need to start your very own aquarium" are examples of checklists. These are easy to create and automate.

Informative newsletters sent out on a schedule are also popular. Offer someone a free subscription to your newsletter if they sign up. Then, send out newsletters on a timely schedule and pack them with great content. Spin them to sell a product or service that you offer, as well.

SELLING CONTENT

When you sell content, you are selling information to people who want to learn more. The most popular forms of content selling include online courses, consultations, information sessions, eBooks, and newsletters. People can sign up for these informational services and pay a fee that you set.

If you can establish yourself as an authority with great, riveting blog content, then people will want to learn everything that you can teach. You can market your information and get many people to sign up. In this day and age, often heralded the "Information Age," selling information is a fantastic way to make money.

To successfully sell information, you must offer something that people can't get on their own. Or at least make people think that they can't get the information on their own. In your marketing, tell people that you have developed a special system for something pet-related.

Always be honest with selling information because you never want to lie to your following. If you do, your followers will figure it out, and their trust will be gone.

Marketing must include video presentations, where you give away about twenty percent of your "system." A great example of information video marketing that I witnessed recently was a vet who created a lengthy video promising to divulge secrets that the pet food industry won't tell you.

He spent a few minutes discussing his veterinary practice and experience, and then he launched into how most dog foods don't offer proper nutrition. He even covered a bit about how canines are meant to eat.

But instead of sharing the true secret of his pet food formula, he instead invited you to sign up for his course on canine nutrition and get twenty percent off of his powdered formula.

People also tend to love systems with steps. "Seven Steps to Reducing Anxiety in Dogs" would be a great example of a course if you decide on offering courses. Breaking things down into a neat system that works is appealing to people. They will be willing to purchase information that can help them tackle problems with their pets in easy-to-follow steps.

Create an organized course where you offer good information and a system. Write the content and add videos. Then market it with a video that gives away a tiny bit of the secret, establishes your authority, and promises people that their pets will benefit enormously from the information contained inside.

Only after all of the marketing should you reveal the price. Make people want the course before you ask for money. People will be more inclined to buy the content if they are already curious about it.

PAID PRODUCT REVIEWS

Free pet products and even payments for posting reviews? Sign me up!

A fantastic way to monetize your pet blog is to offer pet product reviews. Companies will want you to promote their products, as word of mouth works very efficiently as a form of advertising. They will gladly send you free products to review. Many will even pay you to post those reviews!

You can approach companies and ask them about a paid review. Offer to post a flattering review in exchange for a free product, or some other arrangement.

This practice can broach into unethical territory pretty quickly. Don't try a product and then promote it if you didn't like it. Don't promote unsavory companies, either.

It is far better to post positive reviews about products that you have already tried. If you don't like a product some company sends you, you can cancel the deal instead of posting a good review that encourages your reader to buy something horrible.

Your readers trust you and look to you as an authority. Your reviews can drive them to buy something. Please don't violate that trust for money.

Furthermore, you can get into affiliate marketing and use affiliate links in your reviews to drive leads. Read on to see how to transfer reviews into actual money!

AFFILIATE MARKETING

When you post an affiliate link in your blog, you are basically referring people from your blog to another company. As people click on these links and give their business to the companies you refer them to, you make said businesses money.

They will kick you some of the profits in the form of a commission per lead. This is called affiliate marketing, and it is a super common monetization strategy for bloggers.

Another great thing about affiliate marketing is that some companies will give you exclusive discount codes to offer your readers. Everybody loves discounts.

As you advertise a twenty percent off code on your blog, people will be more inclined to click on the link and redeem the code. Therefore, you drive yet more people to an affiliate company.

To get started with affiliate marketing, you want to create affiliations with certain companies. Sometimes, companies will approach you, asking if you might be willing to promote their products on your site. Other times, you can reach out to companies through cold emails and start an affiliation.

Of course, use discernment as you do this. You don't want to be supporting a company that engages in unethical animal treatment or sells lead-poisoned pet products made in unregulated foreign companies, for example.

The companies you work with represent who you are, so a bad company can really sour your reputation online. Be sure to research a company to see if it fits your ethical code before you agree to an affiliation. Look at its reviews, its Better Business Bureau rating, its ingredients, its manufacturing process, and its social media reputation.

You also want to recommend companies that you have actually used. That way, you are posting relevant information about it in your promotions.

If you have never used a product, you should not market it, as you are basically promoting something that you know nothing about. That can easily show in your writing. Plus, you don't want to promote something that doesn't actually work!

Think of a few products that you use. Or think of some that would be in line with your niche that readers could really benefit from. Approach those companies. Usually, on their website footers, you can find a link for "Affiliates" or some such word. If you can't find this, you can send a cold email, which I talk more about in this chapter.

Finally, you can join an affiliate network, which connects you with lots of companies looking for affiliate marketing. ClickBank, Amazon Associates, ShareASale, and CJ Affiliate are a few affiliate networks you can try.

Affiliate marketing generally makes you more money than simply hosting ads. You must partner up with a company's affiliate program and then use your unique ID in posts, banner ads, or newsletter links that you send out. You can also post a product review promoting a product or service with your affiliate link.

In addition, you must create a disclosure page on your blog that tells readers what you are doing and how you are making commission on the companies you promote.

You must also include terms of service and a privacy policy. Simply look up sample pages and add them to your site. All of this legalese is imperative to build trust in your readers and avoid potential legal squabbles.

WordPress does have some restrictions on what products and links you can promote. Check with your platform to ensure that you are allowed to run certain affiliate marketing campaigns.

Also, if you start advertising lots of affiliate businesses, you will find that all of the banners and ads can slow your site down. That's when you should visit your plug-ins menu and find an affiliate plug-in.

This is not necessary if you are just hosting one or two affiliate ads, but if you are hosting more, be sure to get a plug-in to help you stay organized and fast.

COLD EMAILING

If a company does not belong to an affiliate network or have an affiliate key on their website, you can reach out in person.

You really want to sell yourself and your blog to this company so that they want to work with you. Therefore, send a polite and well-written email that you have thoroughly proofread with ProWritingAid (Resources).

At the top, have your name, company, and blog URL. Then begin with "Dear [insert company name]." Doing this shows who you are and that you know who you are writing to.

Below that, write an attention-getting headline. Something controversial can work. Or you can use something friendly, like "Let's Make Each Other Some Money!" Even something cute, like a picture of your pet and a headline about "Your Pet Shampoo Makes My Pooch Happy!"

The last thing you want to do is send an email with a boring headline. The goal here is to get someone's attention!

Next, launch into a story. Talk about how you started from nothing and gained a million followers, or something else relevant. Show this company that your blog is successful, or about to be, and how they can benefit from partnering with you.

Mention your demographic. "To those who live in small apartments with big dogs, I am an advocate that you can do it! I believe you are, too." Show similarities between your demographic and the company's.

You want to personalize the email to show that you did research into the company and you are not just mass emailing—even if you are! Each cold email you send needs to be personally addressed to the company and mention facts you know about it.

Next, offer the company value. Say that you can generate significant traffic on their site with an affiliate link. Maybe mention a problem they have with marketing and how you can help. You want to show a company that you will scratch their backs if they scratch yours.

Finish with a bold call to action. "If you want to make money and gain traffic, you should consider partnering with me!"

Conclude with, "Thank you for taking the time to read this. I can't wait to hear from you." This ending is key. It implies with certainty that you will hear from the company, which makes the recipient of your email more likely to actually write you back. Plus, it makes the recipient feel appreciated for reading your email.

Close with something like "Sincerely" or "Regards." This makes your email professional. Then type your name and add a signature.

ADVERTISING

Companies will pay you to host ads to their businesses or products on your site. Join Google AdSense and post your site's keywords.

Then, merchants can bid on your keywords and pay you every time someone clicks on their ads. Google will take a small cut and send the rest of the money to you.

To add Google AdSense to your blog, follow these steps:

Step 1: Set Up an Account

Visit Google AdSense. If you already have a Gmail account, you can use that to sign up with no hassle. If you already use YouTube or Blogger AdSense, you can get into your account and submit an application with your blog's URL to change it to a WordPress account.

Step 2: My Ads

Click on "My Ads." Then hit the "Add New Ad Unit" button. From there, select the type of ad you want to feature. A video ad, a text ad, an in-article ad—there are a wealth of options here. Text and display ads are ideal.

Step 3: Customize the Ad

Specify the size and colors. Use the "recommended" ones, as these are the ones with typically higher payouts. Then name it. The name really doesn't matter, so use whatever you think will help you remember what the ad is for.

Google will then find an ad for you. If it doesn't, then you can collapse the ad. Then hit save, and you will see a code. Copy and paste this into your notepad on your computer.

Step 4: Add to WordPress

Go to your WordPress dashboard and click on "Widgets." Then drag and drop your "Custom HTML" widget to the appropriate spot on your site and copy and paste the ad code. Save the changes and view your site to ensure that the ad displays correctly.

You can also look into plug-ins that help you place the ad better. Again, I recommend Avada (Chapter 4), as this theme makes it extremely easy to add this step.

Step 5: Don't Click on Your Own Ad

You might be tempted to generate a little extra moolah by clicking on your own ad or getting family and friends to do this for you. But Google has eyes everywhere, and it can tell when you do this. You can get banned from the system for trying to cheat it. Not good!

ONLINE STORE

A blog is a fantastic marketing opportunity if you have a business. Simply create an online store through a WordPress plug-in and promote your store with your blog. Each of your blog posts should mention one of your products or services.

For example, maybe you created your own horse stall bedding. You should create a store that sells your product. Then write articles about horse care and stable maintenance.

Mention your product and include lots of links to your online store throughout these ads. Also, dedicate an entire page to your store and offer videos and articles supporting your product.

I did this for centerforpetlossgrief.com. I created my own store with inexpensive PDFs for people to purchase. I also wrote a number of blogs for each product, and within that blog I provided an internal link (Chapter 4) so the reader would be directed to that particular product in my store.

Or, if you own a store of the brick-and-mortar variety, use your blog to promote it. Include a great "About Us" page (Chapter 4) that highlights your business's purpose, industry, mission, and history. Include business hours, address, social media, and phone on each page. Have a "Contact Us" page, as well. If you can, upgrade your store to include a digital store, as well, in order to reach a broader audience.

Offer subscribers a newsletter. Then, send out relevant content in the newsletter, with a bit about your products or your store at the bottom of each one.

Be sure to mention sales and specials, and try to offer new subscribers a coupon code. That is fantastic marketing that can reach many people.

WRAP-UP

Now you know how to monetize your blog! Blogs require work, but the work can be fun, inspiring, and profitable. By using affiliate links, ads, and an online store, you can generate passive income, even while you watch TV or take a vacation! Put in the work and then see the monetary rewards that pour in.

A monetized blog is truly rewarding. As long as you approach companies about ads and affiliate partnerships, stay on top of marketing emails to your subscribers, offer comprehensive reviews, and promote your own business, you can generate a nice passive income. It is both easy and fun!

You have now created a blog, customized it, worked on gaining a following, and started the process of monetization. Did you ever think you would get this far?

Well, you have! As you reach the end of this book, I hope that you have learned a lot. You have all of the tools and skills necessary to become a blogger. Welcome to the wonderful world of blogging!

But before you go—make sure you check off each action step below. These will keep you on track as you monetize your blog.

ACTION STEPS

Listed are the steps I covered in this chapter. Use the action steps as a checklist as you proceed with creating your blog. Refer back in this chapter to gain more detail when you are ready for the tasks outlined below.

Six Steps to Monetizing Your Blog

Step 1: Send out lead magnets to your email subscribers. Offering something free makes people want to spend more!

Step 2: Sell what you know. The Information Age makes selling information a big hit!

Step 3: Review products. You at least get free products, and maybe a check!

Step 4: Host affiliate links. Email companies or join their affiliate programs. Become part of an affiliate network.

Step 5: Host ads with Google AdSense. Then sit back and watch the money pour in as people click on your ads!

Step 6: Host an online store. This is a great place to sell your products or advertise your business.

PEP TALK!

A blog is a fun and rewarding way to get your ideas out there before an audience and generate a little (or a lot!) of money on the side.

Your blog is a vehicle for publishing your ideas, promoting your views, generating business, and building a brand that people love and trust. It's also a great way to make friends and network with other people.

I can't be prouder of you! You have created a blog with meaningful posts. You have found hosting, started a site with WordPress, created some content, and started building a social media brand. As you market yourself across the web, you will see your email list grow and your readership double, triple, and so on!

Depending on your niche, blogging can be a viable way to make a living in today's era. Take advantage of this opportunity to do something both fun and impactful to earn money. The freedom and expression that a blog gives you cannot be rivaled by traditional business.

Whether you want to talk about your favorite pet or give your brick-and-mortar business a leg up, a blog is the way to do it. You will reach many people and make a name for yourself. Using the tips in this book, you will be able to launch yourself into an extraordinarily large audience.

As you can see, starting and running a blog is relatively straightforward. You don't need to be a published author, a pet expert, or a computer whiz to succeed at blogging.

With a few new skills and your passion, you can create a rock-star pet blog that garners a huge following. You can enjoy great success just by being you!

Pet lovers across the world turn to the Internet for meaningful connections, advice, and products. You can tap into a massive market of like-minded people just by offering what you are naturally good at: your own ideas!

I wish you great success and happiness on your journey in the pet writing industry. You can be successful as long as you put your mind to it. A blog is not out of reach for anyone.

> *Follow along with this book to create a riveting pet blog that people will love to read!*

Warmly,

Wendy Van de Poll

July 25, 2019

GLOSSARY

CPanel - is a web based hosting control panel provided by many hosting providers to website owners allowing them to manage their websites from a web based interface. This program gives users a graphical interface from which they can control their portion of the Unix server.

Blog - Blog posts are the fundamental of a blog. Every blog on the internet consists of different blog posts written by the blogger. ... Blogs (and blog posts) can be shared on social networks (Twitter, Facebook, Google+) and people can leave comments under the blog posts in order to start meaningful conversations.

Captcha - A CAPTCHA (a backronym for "Completely Automated Public Turing test to tell Computers and Humans Apart") is a type of challenge-response test used in computing to determine whether or not the user is human.

Hashtags - A hashtag is a label for content. It helps others who are interested in a certain topic, quickly find content on that same topic. A hashtag looks something like this: #wendyvandepoll.com or #dogsoninstagram. Hashtags are used mostly on social media sites. They rocketed to fame on Twitter.

Internal Links - a type of hyperlink on a webpage to another page or resource, such as an image or document, on the same website or domain. Hyperlinks are considered either "external" or "internal" depending on their target or destination. Internal is a link to a page or post within your blog. External is a link out to a website other than your own.

Keyword/ Short-tailed Keyword – Short tail keywords are search phrases with only one or two words. Their length makes them less specific than searches with more words. "Pet" (one word) is an example of a short tail keyword, whereas "holistic raw cat food" (four words) is a long tail keyword.

Long-tailed Keyword/ Keyword Phrase - A keyword phrase is two or more words typed as a search query. For example, "What is the best way to feed my senior cat" is a good example of a keyword phrase.

Meta Description - The meta description is a snippet of up to about 155 characters – a tag in HTML – which summarizes a page's content. Search engines show the meta description in search results mostly when the searched-for phrase is within the description, so optimizing the meta description is crucial for on-page SEO.

Page – A WordPress Page is considered static and a type of timeless content. For example, the "About" or "Contact" pages of your website/blog do not need a published date to be displayed.

Post – A WordPress Post is a dynamic article that has a published/updated date and is displayed on the blog page. If you want to publish a blog post about anything in your niche, or an announcement, you should use a post.

SEO - SEO or Search Engine Optimization is the name given to activity that attempts to improve search engine rankings. In search results Google™ displays links to pages it considers relevant and authoritative. Authority is mostly measured by analyzing the number and quality of links from other web pages.

Server – A server is the central and usually the largest and most powerful computer in a network that houses the server software. It stores and manages the common network data and supplies it to the individual clients. It provides shared services such as access to the Internet and other networks, faxing, printing, etc. They function as file servers that receive, store, and send files, web servers that store webpages, and mail servers that receive, store, and forward emails.

SSL Certificate - An SSL Certificate (Secure Sockets Layer), also called a Digital Certificate, creates a secure link between a website and a visitor's browser. By ensuring that all data passed between the two remains private and secure, SSL encryption prevents hackers from stealing private information such as credit card numbers, names and addresses.

Website - a group of World Wide Web pages usually containing hyperlinks to each other and made available online by an individual, company, educational institution, government, or organization.

WHOIS - WHOIS (pronounced "who is") is an Internet service used to look up information about a domain name. While the term is capitalized, "WHOIS" is not an acronym. ... Whenever an individual or organization registers a new domain name, the registrar is required to make the registration information publicly available

RESOURCES

A FREE GIFT

Create Your Winning Pet Blog Checklist
https://pages.convertkit.com/be91f83834/446826a572

AFFILIATE SITES**

ConvertKit - email provider
https://mbsy.co/convertkit/50525366

ProWritingAid - editing software
https://prowritingaid.com/?afid=6812%27%3EProWritingAidEditingTool

Siteground - website host
https://www.siteground.com/?referrer_id=7509454

AVADA ONLINE INSTRUCTION

Avadaphile
https://avadaphile.com

EMAIL PROVIDERS

Mailchimp
https://mailchimp.com

WENDY VAN DE POLL

KEYWORD SEARCH

Ubersuggest
https://neilpatel.com/ubersuggest

Wordtracker
https://wordtracker.com

Google Keyword Planner
https://ads.google.com/home/tools/keyword-planner

MONETIZATION

Amazon Associates
https://affiliate-program.amazon.com

CJ Affiliate
https://cj.com

Clickbank
https://clickbank.com

PHOTOS

Pixabay
https://pixabay.com

Librestock
https://librestock.com

Deposit Photos
https://depositphotos.com

SERVICES

Upwork
https://upwork.com

Fiverr
http://fiverr.com

SOCIAL MEDIA ORGANIZATIONAL TOOLS

Agora Pulse

https://agorapulse.com

Buffer

https://buffer.com

Hootsuite

https://buffer.com

Later

https://later.com

ShareCount

https://sharecount.com

The **three recommended sites are products that I use and highly recommend. They are affiliate links which means if you purchase the product, I receive a small commission (which helps me greatly as an author.) You are not charged more because of the affiliate link.

ACKNOWLEDGEMENTS

I would like to thank all the animals who have trusted me to be their advocate and voice. They inspire me to be the best human I possibly can.

Many thanks go to my followers, students, and clients. Thank you for pushing me to write this book and the others that will follow in this series. It takes a team to put together a book and I would like to extend my appreciation to all that have helped along the way.

A huge hug goes to my husband, Rick. He is a remarkable animal lover and human being who dedicates his life to the animals and the environment. He inspires my soul. You can find his books on Amazon, as well.

ABOUT THE AUTHOR

Animals are Wendy Van de Poll's passion. Any chance she gets she is hiking with her dog, observing wildlife in her backwoods, and listening to their wisdom.

Wendy Van de Poll is an award-winning and International best-selling author of thirteen books and counting. She has been blogging since 2000 and has created five successful blogs. With her success she is passionate about helping others achieve their writing goals.

Wendy has helped people start their own blogging sites. Her clients describe Wendy as a "dedicated partner who helps get your ideas down on paper, your work (blog or book) in print, and in the hands of readers who want more."

She is the founder of the CenterforPetLossGrief.com. Her website and blog provide a safe place for dedicated pet parents and pet professionals who want support and guidance with pet loss grief, hospice for pets, and coping with the loss of their pets.

Wendy is a certified end-of-life and grief coach and a tested animal communicator and medium.

She holds a Master of Science degree in wolf ecology and behavior and has run with wild wolves in Minnesota, coyotes in Massachusetts, and foxes in her backyard.

Wendy also coaches people who want write their own books about their pets and other topics.

Her articles can be seen on:

Medium.com: https://medium.com/@wendyvandepoll

Center For Pet Loss Grief, LLC: https://centerforpetlossgrief.com

Wendy Van de Poll, Bestselling Author, Influencer, Animal Advocate: https://wendyvandepoll.com

Pet Blogging 101:
How to Start a Riveting Pet Blog and Gain Loyal Followers

THANK YOU!

As the author of this book, I appreciate you buying and reading it. I hope you found the information useful and you now are on your way to creating a beautiful blog to share with others.

I would be grateful if you would leave a helpful book review, either with your favorite book distributor or with Amazon.

Thank you,

Wendy Van de Poll, MS, CEOL

Best-selling and Award-winning Author, Writing Coach, Speaker

www.wendyvandepoll.com

For all of Wendy Van de Poll's books, please visit:
https:amazon.com/author/wendyvandepoll

ALSO BY WENDY VAN DE POLL

THE PET BUSINESS SERIES
Pet Blogging 101

Pet Jobs 101

Pet Writing 101

PET BEREAVEMENT SERIES
My Dog Is Dying: What Do I Do?

My Dog Has Died: What Do I Do?

My Cat Is Dying: What Do I Do?

My Cat Has Died: What Do I Do?

Healing a Child's Pet Loss Grief

The Pet Professional's Guide to Pet Loss

HUMAN-ANIMAL BOOKS
Animal Wisdom: Conversations From The Heart Between Animals and Their People

FREE BOOK
Healing Your Heart From Pet Loss Grief

CHILDREN'S PICTURE BOOKS
The Adventures of Ms. Addie Pants Series

WENDY VAN DE POLL

The Rescue

The Ice Storm

New Friends

Off to School

To receive notification when more books are published, please go to:

https://WendyVandePoll.com

We will add you to the mailing list after you download your free gift.

You can also find my books on Amazon:

https://amazon.com/author/wendyvandepoll

www.ingramcontent.com/pod-product-compliance
Lightning Source LLC
Chambersburg PA
CBHW060453080526
44584CB00015B/1420